What Teaches a Flower to Bloom?

GLADYS ADISA ERUDE

Worlds Unknown Publishers

Copyright © 2020 Gladys Adisa Erude.

All rights reserved. Published by Worlds Unknown Publishers.

No part of this publication may be reproduced, stored in retrieval system, distributed, or transmitted in any form or by any means, including photocopying, recording, or other electronic or mechanical methods, without the prior written permission of the publisher, except in the case of brief quotations embodied in critical reviews and certain other noncommercial uses permitted by copyright law. For permission requests, write to the publisher, addressed "Attention: Director, Permissions Department," at the address below.

ISBN: 978-1-7356327-7-3 (Paperback)
ISBN: 978-1-7356327-9-7 (E-book)

This book is a work of fiction. Names, characters, places, and incidents are either the product of the author's imagination or are used fictitiously, and any resemblance to actual persons, living or dead, business establishment, event or locales is entirely coincidental.

Printed in the United States of America.
First printed edition 2020.

www.wupubs.com

This book is dedicated to Fionora Kadenge, my mother, and the woman who made me what I am today.

CHAPTER 1

Thriving on His Grace

*For you created my in-most being.
You knit me together in my mother's womb.
I praise you because I am fearfully
and wonderfully made.
Your works are wonderful, I know that full well.
—Psalms 139:13-14*

When I say that I believe that I'm special, truly and wonderfully made, I'm not referring to my outward beauty or any remarkable talent that I may process, though I do believe that I'm special in my own way by God's grace. Looking back at the journey I have made and the road that has brought me this far, I believe that God had a special purpose for my life all along. That is why I was able to make it through everything that I have. He in His grace has enabled me to. I therefore give glory to His name, before everything else.

My roots lie in western Kenya; what was then Kakamega district but is now in Vihiga County, a Village called Tigoi in the Tiriki region. I'm the second-to-last of the surviving children of Benson Kirigano Mireho and Finora kadenge. I must have inherited an immense measure of stoicism from this strong couple, who endured a lot throughout their marriage. The worst they had to endure was the loss of most of their children in infancy. The biggest loss a parent can encounter is the death of a child, especially when this happens before they have had the chance to enjoy the fruit of their womb for enough time. These deaths seemed to follow a certain pattern: two children would die before the third survived. The first two of my siblings died before my sister Selina came along and survived. Then the two that followed her also passed on in infancy before my other sister Truphena survived. After her came two others who passed on before I was born. Then, after me, came Agnes, and my mother had a miscarriage afterwards. Unfortunately, Agnes passed on too. So, of the eleven children my parents had, five boys and six girls, I was privileged to be among the three girls that survived into adulthood. If that is not special, I ask what is?

I grew up as the last born of these girls because I was the last of the "survivors." I believe that God allowed me to survive because He had a special purpose for my life. I'm like a seed that was rooted in sand and gravel, yet God permitted me to grow and blossom, harsh grounds notwithstanding.

I come from the Maragoli community, which is a sub-tribe of the vast Luhya community. In my culture, it is believed that if a parent loves their children too much, they will die or face some other calamity. That aspect of the culture manifested itself especially with my parents, who experienced the heartbreak of losing most of their children in infancy. An intricate naming ceremony is usually held for children whose predeceasing siblings have passed on. Their grandfather would choose names for them that would portray them as ugly, valueless, or unloved—like Hyena, Ant, or Insect. It was believed that this averts death by tricking the death spirit into believing that the child is too worthless for it to be taken away from the parents. My eldest sister, Selina, is therefore also called 'Hyena' (Mbiti), and it was believed that her name helped her to survive childhood, but she later changed it to Makungu, which was the name of our maternal grandmother.

Traditionally, a man is not considered to have children unless he has sons. So, to keep up his place in the community, my father later married our second mother, who was called Safina. In my society, there are no such terms as "stepmother" or "step-sibling.". Every woman your father marries is your mother, and every child they have your true sibling. We were therefore raised by two mothers, and my other mother's three sons and two daughters became my siblings too. They were Maria, Dorcas, Jairus, Javan, and Laban.

The closeness I enjoyed with all my siblings persisted into adulthood. The three of us who are still alive—Truphena, Laban, and I—are still very close and still consult each other on every matter.

Growing up, Javan was special to me because he was closest to me in age, and we developed a closer friendship. I was timid during my childhood, because of the trauma I had experienced, no doubt, and therefore got bullied a lot. He was my bodyguard at school and beyond. He would deal mercilessly with anyone who dared to bully me. He had the exceptional ability to throw a stone without missing. Another thing about him was that he was born with a birth defect. His ears did not develop properly, and he had a hearing defect.

He overcame this challenge, though, and managed to attend a normal school because, at that point, there were no special schools that my parents knew of. He managed to learn the basics of reading and writing. Unfortunately, at the age of seventeen he was struck by polio, which left him paralyzed from the waist down. Despite all that, he exhibited a spirit of resilience and strength beyond measure. He died much later at the age of fifty-six after a valiant battle with cancer.

I wouldn't talk about my family without mentioning that my father had a unique upbringing too. My grandfather, Mireho, was a man ahead of his times as far as raising his children was concerned. My father's mother died when he and his sister Adisa, whom I was named after, were very young: four and two respectively. She was a victim of dysentery, which was rampant in those days due to the unsanitary conditions people lived in. There weren't any bathrooms—not even pit-latrines—and people used the bushes or any secluded place near their houses to answer nature's call. To make matters worse, they watered their livestock in the streams from which they drew water for drinking and other purposes. They used the same watering spots to bathe and do their laundry as well.

Instead of doing what everyone expected for a man living in those times and marrying another woman to raise his young children, my grandfather decided to raise them by himself until they were in their early teens. Only then did he marry beautiful woman whose name was Lydia, whom everyone called M'ma (mother) except for my father who always called her 'Mama'. She was physically beautiful, especially the neatly arranged teeth that gave her the prettiest of smiles, and she also had a beautiful soul inside her. She was like a cool shade in our home, from the harsh sun of my mother's constant beatings and harsh disciplinarian ways. She had been married before. I later developed a close friendship with her and she confided in me as if to an equal even though I was just a child and her step-granddaughter.

Her abusive former husband had accused her of conceiving her first-born daughter Okinda with her own father! This was despite the fact that he had given her kinsfolk a goat—the ritual "fine" that one paid when he proved that his bride was still a virgin. When a woman was forced out of such a marriage, she was subject to terrible stigma, as it was said that she had been 'chased away'. She was forced to leave without her children, who customarily remained with her former husband. If she ever remarried, it was always to a widower. That was how she came to be married by my grandfather.

In my grandfather, she found someone who truly loved her, despite the fact that traditionally, Maragoli men were not expected to openly show such affection for their wives, although this now has changed, of course. He expressed his immense love by always treating her well and providing for her to the best of his ability.

Likely due to genetic factors that my people didn't then have the knowledge to diagnose and treat, three children that my grandfather had with Lydia died in early childhood. Several survived into adulthood, though.

My father was a very humble man. We always took advantage of his humility when we had been spanked by our mothers for making mistakes. If my father found any of his children crying, he refused to eat. He said that it was the trauma of having lost his mother when he was very young that made him to not want to see children suffering in any way. My mother was the disciplinarian in the family, but she was also deeply religious and wanted all her children to follow suit.

As a child, I had a lot of admiration for my Sunday school teacher, Rosa Kanaga. She was very slim and always impeccably dressed and turned out. She and her husband lived in Nairobi where they were employed as servants to a British family. Having learned the ways of the whites—their mannerisms, their eating habits, and their hygiene—she transferred this knowledge to the African women in the village. Most of all, she was the best Sunday school teacher one could have. She gave me a Christian spirit that never left me. She was sweet and kind. She made the children she taught feel guilty when they did something contrary to her teachings.

We never missed church because Rosa gave us candy and also pictures of Jesus and the Angels. Besides that, each one of us got a rose blossom after church. Those things may seem small, but to a child they meant the world. Our Sunday school was full to the brim because of the way the teacher handled the children. Most of us ended up being very good Christians in life. Apart from the gifts the teacher gave us, it was the only time one had to wear the only Sunday best clothes and show off. Sunday best clothes used to be just one attire, worn every Sunday. This meant that immediately after you came home from church, you had to take them off and dress again in tattered rags. Clothing for children was bought only once a year, at Christmas, and this practice is still widespread to this day. Shoes were only possessed by the high and mighty. Most kids went barefoot. Nobody cared, and nobody asked his or her parents for shoes. We knew that they couldn't afford them.

CHAPTER 2

Bound by Special Ties

*Behold how good and how pleasant it is,
for brothers to dwell together in unity!*
— *Psalms 133:1*

Children are a very valuable asset in my community. A marriage could not be seen as complete without any. For this reason, parents went to great lengths to protect their children. To counter the high infant mortality rate, many couples had large families so as to increase the odds of some children surviving. My parents, my mother especially, were not the ones to mollycoddle their children. This was reinforced, I believe, by the belief that if you excessively love a child, then the death spirit will be particularly attracted to them. I believe that we were punished more often than other children in our village . . . but my mother did teach us what every parent should teach their children: good etiquette, the fear of God, and generally upright conduct.

The first three children that my grandfather had with my step-grandmother didn't make it out of their childhood, but those born afterwards survived. My father's younger stepbrothers came to see him as a father figure because of the age difference. They therefore became more like our elder siblings than our aunts and uncles. My father was a very humble and honest person who dearly loved his brothers and sisters. He also knew about gender roles long before the word was coined. He made us do the same chores in the home, both boys and girls. Each one of us had a turn of pasturing and watering animals. All of us knew how to cook except my father himself, who didn't care for it.

My father became the father of the entire extended family after his own father, my grandfather passed on. He worked as a craftsman with the PWD (Public Works Department) at that time, mainly doing construction jobs. One of his Asian employers recognized the potential in him and facilitated him to go to a driving school, where he learned to drive trucks. He thus became one of the very first black African drivers, a status that earned him a lot of respect in the community and beyond. He spent just about everything he earned on his brothers' education and upkeep, and they in turn did not disappoint. The oldest of them, Alphayo, qualified to be a medical officer, Samuel became a vet, and the last born, Peter, who was our baby sitter when we were younger, became a mechanic.

Back then, children weren't allowed to eat meat; they just took the soup, as the meat was reserved for the grownups. Our uncle Alphayo, though, would share his meat with us and allow us to eat from the same plate as he, which was very special. But this love was somewhat offset by the fact that he was a strict disciplinarian who would punish us for the smallest mistakes. Samuel, on the other hand, was very soft-spoken. He liked to gather the children around him, teaching us basic etiquette, like chewing with our mouths closed and saying "please" and "thank you."

We spoke the Luhya dialect Lurogoli, which is our language, but our clan extends beyond the boundaries of Maragoli into the rift-valley, where Kalenjin is spoken. As such, my uncles could speak fluent Kalenjin and, in fact, conversed mostly in Kalenjin amongst themselves. Samuel used to teach us some Kalenjin and even gave us Kalenjin nicknames. Mine was Jeptenai and my sister Selina was nicknamed Jeruto, which I later learned meant "one who has been reborn."

Peter was a regular comic, who could do uncanny and hilarious imitations of other people. He was also a great cook, and our parents could rest assured that we would not go hungry whenever they left us with him. Whenever he cooked food that was intended for the adults only, he would put in a lot of chili to prevent us children from even touching it.

A lot of the time, the main meal was supper, and during the day, we mostly ate fruit: oranges, guavas, and pawpaws, of which there was abundance in our compound.

Because my father was the oldest when my grandfather died, he was given the responsibility of making sure that his brothers were properly married, and that meant giving out their bride price. In my culture bride price is given in the form of cows and money. My father did all that for his brothers because marriage brings two communities together. The parents are the ones to meet and discuss bride price but not the two people concerned with the marriage. A wife therefore marries into a community, not just the husband. As much as my father gave away for his wives and the those of his brothers, he didn't insist on it for his own daughters. He placed more value on their happiness than material wealth.

We also had aunties. My father's immediate younger sister, Adisa, after whom I was named, died before I was born. She wasn't survived by any children. One could argue that there was a genetic hereditary illness, perhaps sickle cell anemia that ran in my father's family because of the high number of children that died in infancy. It also could have been the fact that there were no proper health care and postnatal clinics that could provide vaccination for the babies. Another cause could have been sheer ignorance. For instance, diarrhea and dysentery were common, and children would succumb to these because people believed that giving them water to drink would worsen the disease, so they would die of sheer dehydration.

Our step-aunt Okinda, the firstborn of our step-grandmother from her previous marriage, often visited. Her marriage was exogamic, and she would speak her husband's Luo dialect, claiming that she could no longer speak our language. She was definitely not our favorite when we were children because she was very demanding, sending us up and down on errands when we wanted to play. She was a bit distant, and we didn't know much of her family, except two of her daughters—Mariam and Ngasi—who visited often.

Our favorite was her younger sister Freda, who was our step-grandmother's firstborn with our grandfather. Her life was much like what mine turned out to be, as you will later see. She was married to a man called Joseph, who worked as a tailor in Naivasha. That was around the time of the emergency declared by the colonial government in their bid to stop the Mau-Mau freedom fighters.

My uncle Joseph was among the hundreds of Africans rounded up and put in prison for no apparent reason. The prisoners were tortured, beaten, and starved for days until a lot of them died right there in prison, including Joseph. Aunt Freda was six months pregnant at that time, and she later had Elphas. Soon after that, her husband's people started blaming her for bearing an ill omen and causing her husband's death, and she was driven out of her home consequently. She lived with us for eight years until she married a widower also called Joseph, who had two children of his own. They lived and worked in the tea plantations of Nandi hills, but their happiness was short-lived because Freda died while giving birth to their firstborn daughter, who also died a few hours later. The now totally orphaned Elphas was adopted by my mother, thus becoming my brother.

My father's last-born sister was Priscilla. She didn't have much of an appetite and was very skinny as a result. She was the favorite of M'ma who always went out of her way to ensure that she had as much of what she needed as she could provide. Her marriage to a chief was not very happy because he mistreated her so much and later married a second wife before he died. Priscilla, however, lived to a very ripe old age.

All my aunts went to school long enough to be able to read and write. They realized the value of being able to read the letters their husbands (working away from home) wrote from time to time. That saved them from the ordeals that those who were totally illiterate had to face. These could walk for miles just to find someone who could read a letter for them, and sometimes fell victim to charlatans that pretended to know how to read. A particular example of these was a certain lady who was deceived that a letter from her husband said that he was very ill—in fact on his death bed. She sold off all the chickens the family owned and travelled to be at her husband's death bed only to find him hale and hearty. He had only written to inform her that his leave was about to start and he was going to travel to be with her and the children for a while.

Our family was very close-knit. Even when I talk about having favorites, it doesn't mean that we fought. Laughter was everywhere in our family.

Life was good. In those times, children weren't restricted from roaming the village. One could go to any home where there were other children just to play with them. If food was served in that home, the visiting children were invited to join in the meal. Africans tend to be very generous with food. Even now, one is offered food in every home they go, and it's considered disrespectful to refuse. The owner of the home would think you have looked down upon them if you turned down their offer of food while visiting. No matter how full one is, he or she must take a small bite to show that he did not just refuse to eat. M'ma told me that, among Africans, food is considered a communion that everyone present must partake of. I have since read that in the Bible as well.

One admirable aspect of African life, especially in my region, was women breastfeeding each other's babies. It was taboo to express milk and leave it behind for the baby when women went to the market, which took a whole day. If there were two nursing mothers in the village, one would go to the market as one stayed behind to nurse both babies. I am yet to know if there were cases where a mother favored her baby and nursed it more than the other. I came to learn about such cases when I took an African American studies class, where I learned that slave women were forced to nurse their mistresses' babies while their own languished in malnutrition. But that is a subject for another day.

Back to the village life. All houses were mud and grass-thatched huts. Most of them were only divided into two rooms. One room served as a kitchen and bedroom for the mother of the home. The other room was both a living room and contained a bed for the father. A little space was set aside for the cows, goats, and sheep to sleep. Chickens were accommodated under the father's bed. Because such huts were not large enough for the whole family, the boys had their own hut called a *simba,* or if there was an old widower, the boys would spend nights in his hut. This was a time for the boys to get life skills teaching.

The girls were accommodated in an old woman's hut, especially if the woman was a widow, like M'ma. When I was still young, I often heard her tell the bigger girls how to be well behaved and how they should respect people, especially their husbands, when they got married. One lesson that I didn't understand was to tolerate the husband's beatings because culture allowed men to beat their wives. She taught them to be hard workers on the farm because that was where food came from. She taught them about the importance of cleanliness, both with respect to their bodies and their houses. It made me understand why my mother got up first thing in the morning with a broom in her hand. She had to sweep in and around the house, get the animal droppings out, and scoop out the ashes from the hearth. She would also put the house in order before milking the cows and making porridge for breakfast. All those lessons have stuck in my mind. I do not start cooking unless my kitchen is spotless. I also make sure I have washed all the cooking pans before sitting at the table to eat. You can never find a full sink in my house, and that is my motto.

CHAPTER 3

The valley of the shadow of death

*Even though I walk through the shadow of death,
I shall fear no evil, for thou art with me.
Thy rod and thy staff,
They comfort me.
—Psalms 23:4*

The joy and excitement that I have described aside, there was a dark period of my childhood that remains crystal clear in my memory, even though it started when I was only about three years old.

At that time, my uncle Samuel moved to Kakamega town, which is about fifty kilometers away from our home. I have come to believe what psychologists say, that every event that occurs in one's childhood gets recorded on the memory chip of one's mind. People who mistreat children should always take this into consideration.

Uncle Samuel had just married a young woman of about fourteen, and he was just twenty-three. His wife, Lily, must have been afraid of staying all alone in the house when he was away at work. His work involved a lot of traveling, and a lot of time, only Lily and I would be left in the house. For a while, I was their darling. They spoiled me rotten, buying candy, biscuits, and all sorts of treats for me. I easily got tired of those, probably because I was so used to simpler things, but they didn't seem to understand. Normally, a child my age would crave such treats and make a big deal of them. At that time we were inseparable. Lily took me everywhere she went, and when Uncle Samuel was around, all three of us would go out, each of them holding one of my hands.

The fact that we stayed next to a cemetery took me a long time to get used to. I was very afraid of the dead, especially after hearing the stories people told of ghosts screaming and wailing at night in the cemetery.

Another thing I hated Kakamega about was when Lily took me to a neighbor's house for the day when she went somewhere she didn't need to take me along. The woman of the house had three children, all older than me. They were all very mean to me. The children pinched me as the woman would slap me across the face, forcing me to wash her dishes. I was too young to do such chores, but nobody seemed to understand. I never told anybody about what went on in that house because M'ma had told me that it was a sin to tattle.

I don't know how long we lived that way before Lily fell sick. She threw up all the time, and I thought she would die because it reminded me of the death of my sister Agnes. There was no way that I would have known that Lily was expecting a baby. When her tummy started bulging out, I just thought she was eating too much food. Children did not discuss such matters. Children just found babies in their homes and were told they'd been brought by an airplane at night. I wondered why the airplanes were selective and didn't drop some babies at our house for my mother. As children, we went stay at a house where a baby had been "dropped" and even spent nights there. Our mothers let us, knowing that the excitement would soon wear out. Anyway, as Lily's belly grew big, I heard women gossip that she was pregnant.

We later went back home to the village so that Lily would be attended to by the village women when her delivery day came. It should be understood that there were no hospitals in the village. Moreover, it was a sign of bravery to have a baby at home with older women in attendance. To have a baby in a hospital was considered weak. Women, who later received training to be called Community Birth Attendants (CBA) in the late eighties and early nineties, were just local women who helped deliver babies. At the same time, it was believed that a woman expecting a firstborn had to be near their mother or mothers-in-law, who could train them how to breastfeed and generally handle the newborn baby. I'm sure the local midwives knew what they were doing. They even knew that they had to sterilize their hands before touching the baby.

For a sanitizer, they washed their hands in cow pee before using water and soap. Lily's day came, and I woke up to a baby girl who had been dropped by the airplane.

"Didn't you hear it at night?" asked my mother.

I hadn't heard anything, of course, but I lied. As was the custom, the family children moved to Lily and Uncle Samuel's hut for a few days. The baby was a girl named Judy. She became Lily's joy, pride, satisfaction, and attention. Nothing else mattered. But one month after Judy was born, my uncle became ill and the illness turned to insanity.

For about six months, Uncle Samuel wasn't in his right mind. He held my hand all the time, although he was very violent to other people. He never hurt me.

His wife abandoned him. She ran to neighbors' houses for refuge every time she saw him. I remember my mother slapping her one day when she remarked, "Why can't Samuel just die instead of being insane?" That was an unfortunate thing to say. It became the matter of the clan. I hope that as you read this you realize that Africans believe in society; they are social and very communal. Anything happening to one of their own, good or bad, happens to all. The clan converged and passed a verdict that Lily had to be banished to her parent's home for a year.

During my uncle's instability, my father brought in medicine man after medicine man to no avail. In the process, he sold a lot of family livestock to pay for the treatment. He even sold the ten-acre farm he had just bought to pay for Uncle Samuel's treatment. After several months of mental illness, Uncle Samuel slowly regained his sanity. He was accepted back at his place of work, where he resumed his job as a vet. Lily was allowed to come back with a fine of a cow for disrespecting her sick husband. She only came back after Samuel had long been cured and resumed work, this time in Eldoret. After Samuel had settled, he invited his wife and daughter to live with him in his new residence. He insisted that I go too.

Eldoret was a town called Six Four by the British, presumably because it was exactly sixty-four miles from other towns, especially Kisumu and Kakamega. It is within the Rift Valley at the foot of Mount Elgon, and was then surrounded by Kaptagat Forest, a fact that made it a very cold place. The main fuel for cooking was charcoal, which people bought by the sack, just to make sure that they had enough for cooking and to keep warm. The houses didn't have electricity or running water. We drew water from a communal faucet outside, which was built into the wall of what were the communal bathrooms and toilets. The toilets were not very clean, as there were only two—one for the men and one for women and children. These served a population of about one hundred people. Since there was no sewer system at the time, the toilets were just a hole with a pail underneath it.

A person employed to do the job had to come every morning to empty the pails. I can assure you that I did not envy him for that job, neither did I think I could eat from the same plate with him, as is the African custom. There was pee and poop everywhere on the floor of the toilet. No matter how poor one was, they made sure that at least they had some sort of shoes to go to the toilet. The cheapest shoes were made locally out of old car tires. Unfortunately, I had no shoes and had to wade in the dirt to get to the pail that was used to collect human waste.

The estate consisted of twelve units of housing made of brick walls with red brick tiles. They were government houses for government employees of the same grade. Our house was one single room with an extended kitchen. There was only one bed, which was shared by Uncle Samuel, Lily, and their daughter Judy. I slept on the cold floor on a mat and without anything to cover myself except Lily's old dress. The nights were so cold. I would shiver as the wind blew through the cracks beneath the door. Lily, who had loved me so much at one time, had long since transferred her love to her own daughter. I didn't matter to her anymore. She never hid the fact that I was better dead than alive, and to her, I was not a daughter in the African sense, I was but no better than a slave.

The situation became worse, as Samuel still traveled, leaving me with Lily and the baby—not that he did much when he was around. I later came to understand that when people love each other, they don't see the pain caused by one of them to a third party. My nightmare had just begun. Lily beat me up all the time for no apparent reason.

She always looked at me as if I was a boa constrictor or some other vile creature. She pounced on me with kicks, blows, and slaps. She twisted my lips. She held me up by the ears until I thought my ears would fall off. She hit my head on the wall or the concrete floor, and when I bled, the sight of blood sent her into a frenzy of even more violence, as if she was demon possessed. She would put a piece of metal or a knife in the fire only to use it to burn my flesh. I still bear some of the scars, more than fifty years after the fact. The neighbors just watched. I have never understood why the neighbors didn't say anything or try to rescue me. The bystander effect reigned in those days. That was my daily life.

Lily loved food, and my uncle knew how to provide for his family. Every morning, four pints of milk were delivered to the house. There was a man from our village called Javan who worked at a slaughterhouse, and he delivered meat to the house every day, even if the previous day's supply was still untouched. Because there was no electricity and we didn't have a fridge, Lily usually dried her meat so that it didn't go bad. I saw the meat with my eyes, and I even helped in smoking it on an open fire, but she would never allow me to taste it.

She also raised chickens for eggs, which were kept in the kitchen. One of my daily chores was to get up at five o'clock in the morning, open the door for the chickens to get out, then sweep the floor of the kitchen and mop off the chicken droppings, despite only being five years old.

Venturing through the cold, I went to the water faucet to wash dishes and get some water to make tea at that ungodly hour. It took me about thirty minutes to start the charcoal stove outside in the cold, hoping there would be enough wind to blow the fire alive. I brought the stove to the house, grateful that I could warm myself as I made tea for my boss. As soon as she knew the fire was ready, she got up and pushed me outside to stand in the cold, until they had had their tea. I was not allowed to drink any milk in the house. I would make my sugarless cup of strong tea after they were done taking their tea with milk.

As much as all African children yearned for bread, I was not allowed to eat bread. It was for the royal family only but not the slave. In fact, I hardly had enough food to eat at all. I lived on crumbs and burned crusts from pans, which I scraped and ate when I went to clean the dishes at the water faucet. When we had a visitor, she allowed me to eat with others but amid abuses, saying that I was eating like a prostitute. It didn't hurt me as much as the beatings because, one, I did not know the meaning of the word "prostitute," and, two, as long as I had good food to eat, it was ok to be called names. When I continued eating, she snatched the plate from my hand and said the remaining food was for her daughter. Despite all that, I didn't die, and that's why I believe God was with me.

Another scary thing in that house was that Lily believed in witchcraft. She always spent money on witch doctors that made her charms to tie around her children's waists or sew into the hems of their clothing. The witch doctor lived with us while my uncle was away at work.

There was one night, I remember, when a dirty looking man came to spend several nights as usual. He used a razor to make incisions on Lily's and the children's skin, and he rubbed some concoctions into the bleeding cuts. I was hiding under the bed, afraid that he would do the same to me. It was the fear of the pain rather than the sinfulness of the witchcraft. Just as I thought, the witch doctor wanted more patients, which meant more money for him. He called me to come forward to be "treated" but before I answered, it was Lily who retorted, "That one is not worth your precious medicine." They argued for a while, but Lily won.

I didn't know that the Lord was protecting me all the time. After that treatment, things took a downturn. Judy, who had been a vibrant girl, turned into a dull, sickly child. Second-born George didn't heal from the incisions; they got swollen and became septic. The boy I loved so much suffered until he died, as Judy became mentally retarded. I don't know if the witch doctor gave them poison instead of charms to evade witchcraft, or was it God repaying Lily for her cruelty to an innocent child? I still remember George nostalgically. The boy loved me. His mother would only take him from me when he was asleep; most of the time he used to cling onto me and spent nights with me on the cold floor on the mat. Lily would give me a small blanket to cover him. Those were my Christmas nights because I would snuggle with the one-year-old baby in his tiny blanket. At least those nights were warm, when the cold became unbearable. But I had to be very cautious because whenever Lily caught me in the baby's blanket, she would hit me so hard, startling me from my sleep and almost causing me to have a heart attack.

One of the most painful experiences I suffered at the hands of my aunt was being forced to sit in a large basin full of freezing water overnight. That would be my punishment for licking plates after the family members ate, leaving me no food. I scraped crumbs from pans and plates, licking every drop of soup that I could get out of it. The desire to have something in my belly made me suffer pneumonia several times. Later on, when I watched the movie *Killing Fields*, I understood what those people went through. Yet, because my life is a miracle and God watched over me, I didn't die of the pneumonia or hypothermia.

One incident I have never forgotten is when my aunt nearly killed me with a piece of timber with nails protruding all over. I was supposed to watch Judy when her mother left the home, but Judy, now a three-year-old, was stronger than me. I was emaciated for lack of food, plus the daily beatings. When the mother left, Judy would struggle to follow her. I struggled to hold on to her, with George strapped on my back, but she overpowered me and ran out of the house. Lily, who had gone a good distance turned to see me pulling at the stronger Judy and probably mistook my intentions. She picked up a piece of wood with nails on it and came back running. She hit me all over the body as nails tore into my flesh. She didn't care whether the nails poked my eyes, or which part of the body they tore open. I had open skin wounds all over the body when she left and walked away with her daughter like nothing had happened. I couldn't even walk to the house.

After she had gone, a woman who was my sympathizer but could not show it for fear of being accused of prying into other people's welfare, came and took me to the house. My aunt came back in the evening to find me bloody, hungry, and swollen all over. She may have felt guilty because for the time she touched me without beating me. She heated some water, added salt, and cleaned me with a piece of cloth.

By the end of that week I had a terrible fever and all the wounds had become septic. I could hear people discussing me as if I was deaf. One said, "Take her to hospital", yet another said, "The doctor will want to know what happened, and you could be arrested," and yet another one blatantly stated, "Let her die and be buried secretly. You can tell the parents she just ran away." I longed for that death although I didn't know what it was. I just knew people were put in the ground and covered by soil when they died, like they did to my sister Agnes. I was on the verge of despair when God visited in a form of two *mzung*u (white) ladies.

Kenya was still a colony of the British. Once in a while, some white people went through the African estates to see if there were sick people so they could give them medical assistance. Apart from my wounds, I had a terrible skin rash. I spent a lot of time scratching. Now that I know what food does to the body, I understand that all the ailments were a result of my malnutrition. Everybody feared *mzungus*, and so when they came to the house, people were worried. My aunt peed on herself for fear of being arrested, but the ladies were just looking for needy cases.

They looked at me and shook their heads. They couldn't touch me because my wounds were septic, oozing puss, and I looked dirty. They asked the black man who accompanied them to carry me to their car. I was taken to hospital and admitted for a week. I got to sleep in a bed with clean white bed sheets and a blanket. I had three meals a day. I was given lots of milk to drink. Indeed, they were angels sent by God himself because I think I would have died and Lily would have had me secretly buried. They dropped me back home, promising that they would come back to see me.

My clothes were tattered and because I was too young to mend them, I tied knots where they got torn. When I came from hospital, the ladies bought me two beautiful new dresses—the type that we saw *mzungu* children wearing. They bought me underwear and flip flops too. No sooner had they left than my aunt took the dresses away from me and gave them to her daughter, Judy. I was devastated. I cried all the time, but Lily continued with her evil habit of beating me at any and every chance she got.

The beatings were much better compared to the hunger I felt. I was constantly hungry—not that there was no food, but because I did not merit the prestige of eating. I stared as people ate, followed their hands with my eyes as they lifted their hands to their mouths and stuffed their face. I watched, chewing nothing as they chewed food, and swallowing saliva as they swallowed food. I have never understood that kind of animosity. There was plenty of food in our house in Eldoret, but I could not just bring myself down to stealing and eating it. The reason being that I was taught in Sunday school that stealing was a sin, and that those who stole went to hell to burn in Satan's fire forever. I was afraid to die and go to hell although I lived in hell itself. The only thing I could not resist stealing was sugar. I was so hungry and weak that my body craved energy. I just learned this when I went to college and read about nutrition. I must say I lived on the sugar I stole, which gave me some energy and strength to go on.

Apart from the pangs of hunger and physical abuse, I suffered emotional abuse. My aunt was always hurling insults at me until I came to believe that I was ugly, that nobody loved me, that I behaved like a prostitute, and that nobody would ever want to marry me. It was painful to hear that I was too ugly for anybody to want to marry me, because marriage at that time in history was the ultimate goal of all girls. They were socialized to become people's wives from a very tender age. Whatever girls did in those days served the purpose of becoming good wives. Yet here I was being ridiculed all the time. Because of this, when I eventually met my husband at the age of seventeen, and he said that he loved me and that I was beautiful, I didn't believe him. I had never heard the saying that beauty lies in the beholder's eye.

My favorite uncle would come home and, saddened by the state I was in, would send his wife to the shop to buy groceries, so he could get a chance of giving me something to eat, urging me to eat quickly, and not tell his wife that he gave me some food. When I grew up, I came to understand that some people are control freaks, who instill fear in their spouses.

This kind of life would have led me to my death if it wasn't for a man from our village, who worked in the same town, coming to visit my uncle. He found me emaciated, with a skin disease, which had come back to haunt me with a vengeance since the hospitalization. The man, Simon looked at me and kept quiet. It registered in his mind that I needed help. He just visited with my uncle and his wife without uttering a word about me. He decided to travel to the village, straight to my mother. "I thought all your children died except only three girls?" he asked my mother, to which she asked "Why do you ask?" Simon told my mother that her youngest daughter would be buried soon and that she would be left with only two children.

My mother understood it as an adult and was on the way to Eldoret the following morning. She came in unannounced, and luckily enough, we were all there. In fact, she found people eating while I was sitting at a corner, waiting for the leftovers, if any remained. Uncle and Aunt were both shocked to see her. They were all smiles, and I was surprised to hear Lily say that I had refused to eat because I had eaten a lot during the day. Because I had been taught never to talk back to older people, I kept quiet. They prepared food for my mother and obviously she asked me to eat with her. When she saw the speed with which I ate, she left the food for me. I could see her eyes fill up with tears, but she didn't cry.

My mother had brought me a dress and some canvas shoes. If my mother went to school, she would have been a public relations person. She didn't say anything but begged my uncle and aunt to bring me back home because I needed to go to school. I cried when my mother left the following day. The situation changed a bit. Some leftover food would be thrown my way in the same way we throw leftover food at dogs in Africa. It was another two months before I was taken back to the village, but I was.

The years of living under abusive conditions had really traumatized me. I hardly talked. I cried all the time.

I wondered how the sweet loving aunt that I had known in Kakamega had turned into this brutal monster in Eldoret. Was there another reason, apart from transferring the love she had for me to her children? I never got an answer to that question, and I never spoke about the ordeal either. I didn't trust anybody and I never wanted to be touched. I believed that any form of touching could lead to more beatings. That's how it was. The only touch I received at Lily and Samuel's house was when I was being beaten, except the day Lily massaged my body with warm water, after she caused me actual bodily harm with a piece of wood with nails on it.

My self-esteem was so low that I didn't want to say anything to those around me. I feared that they might tell and get me in trouble. I sat in dark corners. I knew I was ugly and that I didn't merit life, which I was made to believe was reserved for the beautiful. I never wanted to eat at the same table, though it was custom in my family to eat from one plate. Lily had once told me that I ate like a prostitute, and so I didn't want my mother to notice how I ate.

My mother, father, sisters, and brothers, uncles, and even my cousins, together with M'ma worked very hard to teach me to love and be loved by family members. I had to learn to trust people again, but the anger had been bottled up inside me. I didn't want anybody yelling at me. That would cause a stream of tears. I would cry at the slightest provocation, which caused a lot of bullying at school. At the age of twelve, I had become so aggressive that I physically fought anybody who tried to tease me. The crying had been replaced by fighting. This again, made me very unpopular with teachers.

I have stated before that my character had changed. I didn't speak much. I didn't play with other children because I was used to being treated like a pariah. It took me time to learn to trust people again—something I haven't fully regained, even to this day.

After two years of learning to accept people back into my life, I made two friends, Gladys and Agnes. We were so close that we helped each other to cultivate our farms in turn. Non-African readers will think of this as child abuse, but that is what we do to become resilient. The youth compete to show their might. Girls carried large containers of water and large loads of firewood. Any girl who didn't know how to dig, carry water, clean the house, and do dishes would be ridiculed and shunned by other girls. If one of us was sick, the others fetched water and firewood for the parents. We were close friends from 1960 to 1962 when Agnes got pregnant and consequently left our group.

I later learned that it was my brother (cousin) Elphas that had gotten her pregnant. By the time I sat for my Kenya Preliminary Examination in eighth grade, in 1965, Gladys had already had Elphas' baby. She ended up marrying him. Agnes got married in South Nyanza, nearly one hundred miles from home, so we lost touch. Gladys is still my friend to this day, though. These two girls helped me reform, learn to talk, and laugh. They made me start to trust people again. The fact that my close friends had babies at a very early age made me fearful. I kept asking myself what I would tell my mother if I got pregnant. Those two cases made me reexamine myself and consider whether I wanted to be a teacher, the most coveted job in the village, or I just wanted to get married and have babies.

The idea of living under the fear of a husband made me shudder. I had seen women with their babies strapped on their backs coming to seek refuge in our home after being beaten by their husbands, as wife beating was a norm in Africa and still is in some places. I opted for education and stayed away from boys. I was proud of my exemplary performance in school, not for myself but for my mother. She rescued me from bondage and I just wanted to make her happy and proud. I worked hard in school, and I was among the top ten in my class.

When I left the residence of Samuel and Lily, my place was taken by my brother Laban. Having been co-wives, our mothers had an implicit jealousy. The mother to Laban wanted one of her own to live in an urban setting too, and I regret to this day not telling my brother that he was walking into the very depths of hell. He has his own story, but this is my story. Because he is a mathematician, he might as well employ my journalism, so that I can help him write his story, and I wouldn't be surprised if it wasn't much different from mine. My brother and I often reminisce about our childhood and why we tolerated such abuse. We both agree that African children are socialized never to raise a voice against their parents or elders. We obeyed orders without questions. Like me, my brother's anger from that time came back to haunt him. He threw a fist punch at anybody who rubbed him the wrong way.

He did well in his studies eventually and became a high school teacher of mathematics and physics, the subjects that I found boring. I had wondered where our anger came from, as we were born of very humble parents. Just recently, I came to understand that continuous childhood abuse can make one over-aggressive and they may even develop bipolar disorder. I thank God for saving me because salvation has cooled my temper down. I now think twice before I react.

A part of my character though, has remained set by my earlier experiences. I listen to people talking to me, as I analyze their speech in my brain. I never take anything for granted or at face value, thanks to my journalistic instincts and training on reading between lines. My character was shaped forever by the abusive life I lived.

CHAPTER 4

School . . . at Last!

> *See that you do not look down on one of these little ones.*
> *For I tell you that their angels in heaven always*
> *see the face of my father in heaven . . .*
> *—Matthew 18:10.*

All the time I was going through a living hell at my uncle's, I longed with every fiber of my frail body to go to school. I wanted to know how to read and write. I wanted to speak English like my uncle. I didn't understand why I stayed home to be beaten all the time when I could be in school. While in bondage in Eldoret, I stood outside every morning watching clean children in uniforms going to school. I saw them coming back in the afternoon and cried silently, lest I be seen, which would have meant a beating.

I remembered my Sunday school teacher telling us that when you pray to God, he will give you what you want. Lying on my cold mat on the floor every night, I whispered to God to make me go to school, and give me some food to eat. It was therefore an answered prayer when my mother came to Eldoret and announced that I needed to go back to the village and start school. After what seemed an eternity—a mere two months, in fact—we finally took a Roadways Nyanza bus, the only one that plied the Kisumu-Eldoret route, back to the village.

Tigoi was a Quaker Mission school, run by the Friends African Mission. One would expect that the teachers in missionary schools were disciplined in the fear of God, but that was not the matter. Beatings were the order of the day. Students would scream with beatings and quit school altogether. Apart from the harsh teachers, many students were bullies too. The combination did not auger well with some students. At the same time, school was voluntary, unless one had parents like mine who wanted their children to go to school. My mother said she once heard a church elder say that those who went to school would replace the whites in offices when the time came. She wanted her children to be among them.

The school was divided into two sections. The primary school section had its own compound, with its own teachers. The uniform was white with green sleeves and a green collar. The boys wore the same shirt colors with khaki shorts. All students wore a badge that said "Tigoi Primary School." Primary education went from first grade to fourth. There was a national exam in fourth grade that one had to pass to join the prestigious intermediate school, whose uniform consisted of purple tunics for girls with a green blouse worn under the tunic so that only the sleeves and the collar were seen. Boys wore both khaki shirt and shorts, and of course the badge. Intermediate ran from fifth grade to eighth, at which point another national exam decided who went to high school and who went to vocational training to become mechanics, tailors, masons, and cooks in white homes, like my Sunday school teacher, Rosa.

The primary school section was comprised of one long mud building thatched with grass. It had large spaces for windows but no shutters. Both the doors and windows were open spaces. The building was partitioned into four rooms, one for each grade. There was a smaller mud and grass-thatched hut on the right-hand side of the tuition block, which served as a staff room. At least that one could be closed because it had a door but no windows—not even open spaces for windows.

It was therefore scary when a teacher asked you to carry books to the office. You never knew who was lying in wait. Bigger girls used to complain that some teachers touched their chests when they took books to the office. It never happened to me because I was ugly, foolish looking, and younger than most of the other girls, or so I thought. The teachers also feared that I would cry. I later came to appreciate the description Lily gave me. It scared off potential sexual abusers because a number of girls ended up getting pregnant, claiming the teachers were responsible. Parents feared and respected teachers too much to do anything when their daughters were defiled, except my mother, who was too assertive. She lived ahead of her time.

The primary school section had three teachers, one of them serving as a headteacher. His name was Barnabas. He was an older man but very kind and understanding. He treated the younger students like his children. At nine years of age, when I started school, I was one of the youngest students, but I had to be in school to avoid going back to Eldoret. Other students were older with ages ranging from ten to twenty. A girl would leave school on a Friday evening, and on Monday morning the teachers received a report that the girl had eloped with a man. That's how old they were. Most of them were very mean, especially if they couldn't write something. They often asked those who knew to do it for them. Refusing to do their bidding would mean a thorough beating for the younger ones. The problem was that they asked us to write letters to their boyfriends as they dictated. Some of the words they wanted us to write cannot be written here.

First-graders spent only two hours at school, from eight o'clock to ten. We only did our numbers and letters, then had physical education. Each class took twenty-five minutes. Sometimes we were taught hygiene, history in the form of folklore, and civics. I grasped everything I was taught with a hungry mind. Because I still did not trust people, I did not have friends. Instead, I spent my time practicing my numbers and letters. I became a target of bullying, but it also put me at the top of the class.

I became a personal interest for the headteacher, Barnabas. He wanted to know how I was doing, and why I was crying because I still cried a lot. The other teachers, Jeremiah and Esther, were not amused. They didn't understand how a foolish-looking girl could be topping the class all the time, performing better than those who had repeated the class several years. Jeremiah would actually beat me for getting all the points, asking whose work I had copied. Most of the time, he made me sit alone at a corner in front of the class to see if I copied anybody's work. He still wasn't sure enough that with my foolish look I could be that smart. I guess he never came across the saying "do not judge a book by the cover."

Teacher Esther taught us religious education. At some point, my mother bought me a New Testament bible, written in my vernacular language, for me to practice reading and come to know the word of God. Teacher Esther borrowed it and left it at home, only to deny that I had given it to her. I cried a lot and later told my mother what had happened. She came to school fuming and demanded the Bible. The worried Esther promised to bring it the next day, which she did, but she became my sworn enemy after that. Despite the beatings, my solace was my high performance. It made me happy and encouraged me to work harder. My favorite moment would be at the close of term or semester, when everybody gathered on parade. Those who topped their classes would be called by name and given presents, which were exercise books and pencils.

During my first-grade year, I couldn't wait to get to second grade so I could write in a book with a pencil. This was because first-graders wrote on small blackboards called slates, using some special chalk made from diatomite, which is mined in Kenya near Gilgil town. The chalk tasted good, so most of the students ate their pieces of chalk and had nothing to write with. I would have eaten mine too, but I did not want to offend my mother, the woman who gave me her full love and support.

By the end of my first year in school, I knew how to put letters together to form words in my vernacular language. The following year, I went to second grade with full confidence. We were given three books each, one for arithmetic, one for vernacular grammar, and the other for combined subjects of history, geography, science, and civics. I had a small bag that my mother sewed for me to carry my books, but I preferred to carry them in the open for everyone to see that I was a second-grader.

In my second-grade class, there was a boy named Osborn. He looked miserable and hungry all the time. He had a large septic wound on his leg, which was stinky. This made other students run away from him. At first, I didn't like him, but later I started having empathetic feelings towards him. I imagined that he could be living in a situation like the one I once lived in. I asked my mother about him, and after describing him, she told me that Osborn's mother had died when he was only two years old. His father, who operated a welding workshop in the shopping centre had married another woman, but the wife did not like Osborn. She mistreated him in the same way that I had been mistreated.

Osborn often slept on an empty stomach after doing all the chores. The wound he had on his leg had been inflicted by the stepmother, who hit him with a hoe. My mother also said that Osborn went from house to house begging for food when he was hungry, but the father would beat him if he knew he did that. On hearing that about Osborn, my heart sank. In class, other students wouldn't share a desk with him because he was stinky. Because of the animosity, Miss Esther harbored towards me from the day I reported her to my mother, she forced me to share a desk with Osborn. Unknown to her, she just might have done him a favor because I was the only one that could be empathetic to his plight.

Osborn suffered from trauma due to having lost his mother and the treatment he got from his father and stepmother. He could not perform in school. He was in second grade but could not even write his name, numbers, and letters. He was always yawning with hunger and tiredness from working too much at home.

My mother started giving me some food to take to him every day. I would get him boiled sweet potatoes or ripe bananas. He was very grateful, hungrily gobbling down the food. When my uncle Alpha came home for a weekend, I told Osborn to come to our home so that my uncle could treat his gaping wound. When he came, my uncle washed the wound with very hot water, then applied some iodine solution and bandaged it, and asked him to come after two days. It did not end there. My uncle made a point of going to talk to his father so he could allow him to come back for treatment, in a reprimanding manner. Osborn's father was not happy about the reprimand.

One day as we came from school and passed his workshop, he asked Osborn and me to come over. We went closer, and he snatched my books from me. First, he looked at Osborn's and found that he did not seem to have got anything right. Then he opened my books and I had gotten all the points. He turned to Osborn and yelled "you good-for-nothing son, how can a mere girl be smarter than you?" He smacked his head, pushed him to the wall, grabbed his head and hit it on the wall repeatedly. Osborn did not even struggle because he was used to beatings. Moreover, he could not fight his father, who was so much stronger. Osborne's father then turned to me and said "And you who goes to report me to your doctor uncle. Do you think you can be smarter than my son?"

He took all my books and ripped them into pieces. I was devastated. It dawned on me that I may have escaped Lily's snare but there were other Lilys around.

After that traumatizing incident, I began to feel that it was wrong for me to be smarter than other students in school because after all, I was a mere girl. People used to say in the village that boys went to school to work and provide for the family. Girls only needed to learn how to make a fire or hold a cooking stick. By the end of third grade, I had slipped back to tenth position from being the top student. The case about Osborn's father ripping my books had to be solved in the church. That is where all the disputes in the community were solved. I did not attend the proceedings, for that reason I wouldn't speculate on what was said. I was given new books in school, and life went on. Osborn later dropped out of school in fourth grade and went to work on the sisal plantations.

Fourth grade was a tough class because students were candidates for the national examinations. Those who passed went to fifth grade in the Intermediate section. That was my desire. I had started learning a little English in third grade. Third grade was also the class in which students learned to use a fountain pen with ink. I made sure I had a drop of ink on my uniform just to show that I was in third grade. I could now read a few English words. I needed to speak some English because it was the only language of instruction in fifth grade. Many students dropped out of school, while others opted to repeat fourth grade. Others even moved back to third grade. I wasn't performing as well as I wanted to, but I was confident about passing the examination. I did and I was accepted at Tigoi Intermediate School, where I got to wear the purple and green uniform.

It was in January of 1962 when I joined the intermediate school. The section had its own mean teachers and rules that made many students just walk out of school. One such rule was speaking English all the time on the school compound. It was difficult because this was a community school where everyone spoke the same language. Moreover, we as students had not mastered the language to use it as a communication tool. To effect the rule, there was something called "disc," a small piece of wood that would be given to one person to start the day by listening to whoever spoke the mother tongue.

At the end of the day, during evening parade, before singing a hymn and saying prayers for the day, the first person would be called upon to say to whom she or he would have given it to. Those who took it were given two strokes of the cane, but those who refused to take it were given eight strokes. Girls got their strokes in the palms of their hands, a very painful experience. The boys were caned on the backside. Some boys put books under their pants, and if discovered, they got sixteen strokes of the cane after removing the books.

Lessons were delivered like in a boot camp. Although school came naturally to me, there were subjects that I did not like. One of them was domestic science, which is now called home economics. It was all about cookery and needlework. I loved cookery, but I couldn't bring myself to hold a needle facing backward to be seen as sewing "like a lady." I would join my pieces with the needle facing forward and the teacher would beat me up for not adhering to their teachings. I wouldn't even touch the stupid hand-driven sewing machine they provided. In the long run, I was to be thrown out of the class forever. Teachers always carried sticks with which to beat students. Nobody talked in class, and nobody laughed. Teachers told no jokes. It was simply teaching. Teachers never interacted with students to know where their interests lay. They expected everyone to understand and score the same.

The tuition fee in the intermediate section was one hundred and fifty Kenyan shillings (the equivalent of one dollar and fifty cents, a shift from the twenty American cents that we paid in primary school. Students were forced to buy material to sew during those classes, but when the material was provided, students were forced to buy what they made, whether they had use for it or not. It was a burden to parents who eked a living to provide for their children's education. Teachers were just too mean, especially when they took students out of class to go cook lunch for them. I felt bad because it was hard for my parents to get the tuition fees, and it was very unfair that I had to leave others studying as I went and cooked for teachers. I decided to rebel, and the teachers were not amused. I was sent to the office and was beaten by all the twelve teachers who were on the staff. I went home with swollen hands, and I had to tell my mother what had happened.

The following day, first thing in the morning, she was at school. It took the headteacher to calm her down. My mother never went to school, and I don't know how she got empowered. She threatened to report the teachers to the school supervisor. She had a long-standing bitterness with teachers of Tigoi Intermediate School, although most of them had been transferred. One teacher had tried to force himself on my sister Selina, who was just fourteen years old then. When Selina wouldn't comply, the teacher had to beat her thoroughly and sent her home, and she had missed school for four days as a result.

My sister had been down with malaria, and everyone knew it. With the malarial weakness and the beatings, my sister collapsed on the way home. An old man in the village stumbled on her and carried her home unconscious. I have said that there were no hospitals in the villages, so proper care wasn't an option. Even so, the villagers knew herbs that could resuscitate an unconscious person. Bearing in mind that my mother had lost several of her children, she decided that Selina was better at home than going to school and being killed. She consequently dropped out of school in fifth grade. She reported the matter to the supervisor and the teacher concerned was fired. Selina knew how to read and write, and her handwriting was very good. It resembled that of my sister Truphena, who was equally smart in school but had dropped out in seventh grade due to peer pressure. By the time I joined fifth grade, both of my sisters were married.

The only other child in my mother's house was Elphas, my Aunt Freda's son. Later on, my brother Laban left his mother's house to come and live with us. My other brothers, Jairus and Javan, stayed with their mother, but we all did things together. I was constantly in the company of my brothers and other cousins. I did what they did, and in the process became something of a tomboy. I learned to fight for my rights whenever I was forced to.

Teachers were sometimes openly biased towards those students who did favors for them. There was one girl whose father lived in Uganda, and her family was considered very rich by the standards then. The girl, Georgina, used to bring teachers food and money, which definitely was the reason that she was made the head prefect. One of her responsibilities was to supervise the pupils who fetched water to be used in school since our school didn't have running water. All the water used by teachers and cleaning the school was brought in by the girls. Georgina was the one who inspected the water containers; if your water container was too small, she would pour out the water, give you a larger container and order you to walk four miles to the stream and back. All this time, other students would be in class learning new things.

If Georgina reported you for being rude, all the teachers would take her side and gang up to punish you. One day I brought in a large container of water but it was only half full because I believed that since it was so big, I had still brought in enough water even though it wasn't full. On inspection, Georgina kicked the pail and spilled all the water, ordering me to pick it up and go to the stream. Other students whose water had been poured out obeyed, but I told her I wasn't going to let her use my tuition while I fetched water. I went to class and sat at my desk. She couldn't do anything during class hours but announced on parade that I had rallied my brothers to beat her up, a lie that infuriated me so much I just shot up and yelled; "You may be very tall, very light-colored, and very rich, but I cannot involve my brothers in my fight with you!" With that, I vented all the bitterness that had accumulated in me over her mistreatment.

After school, she started a fight with me. I was shorter than her, but I jumped up, caught her neck and brought her down, beating her up with all the pent-up fury inside me. A teacher who was going home heard the commotion and came back with a switch. He hit me twice on my back until my uniform was ripped and the switch caught my skin where it was exposed by the rips. I left Georgina, turned on the teacher, snatched the switch from his hands and whacked him several times. Meanwhile, Georgina got a chance to run away. Realizing that she was running, I left the teacher and ran after her. It all happened on a Friday evening and I expected to be sent away from school the following Monday. My mother was there with me to complain about the fees she pays, only for her daughter to be sent to fetch water. She made a scene and because people knew her capabilities, the matter just fizzled out. I didn't talk to Georgina until 1995 when we met in China in 1995 for the 4th UN Women's Conference. We both laughed about it, and I guess without saying it, we forgave each other.

At least I made some friends in intermediate school, and one of my closest friends was a girl called Florence. We used to go to each other's homes for lunch. I had tried to be friends with a girl called Stella, when we were still in primary school. There was this time she came to me with a pencil, which she convinced me to help her steal. We scraped off the color of the pencil, and she told me to keep it and then reported me to the teacher for stealing the pencil! Of course, the pencil was found in my bag, totally cutting off any chances of pleading innocence; the evidence was there. I was therefore branded a thief, which made me cry so much. After that incident, I never made friends with anyone else apart from Osborn, whom I empathized with. Florence was different though. She was disciplined, and I used to help her do her homework since I was still quite bright in my studies.

There was a teacher called Henry who tried to separate us by claiming that I looked too foolish to be that smart, and that I must have been copying Florence's work. Like Jeremiah and Esther, he put my desk at a corner to sit alone and see whose work I would copy. They were embarrassed because they soon came to know who copied whose work after all. I had another friend called Grace, but one day we differed and fought over ink and in her anger, she said that I was black like charcoal. That hurt me so much that I physically fought with her. I was told she went home bleeding from the head, but I didn't know how much I hurt her. Having grown up and studied psychology, I now realize that I was angry with everybody and was lashing back at them for what I had gone through.

One incident that made me hate teacher Henry for a long time was the death of my cousin Francis, who I'd been very close to. He caught malaria and died five days after. Malaria was not considered a disease in my community; it was so rampant that people just ignored it. The moment one threw up green bile juice, it was considered a sign that one was recovering, and everyone gave a sigh of relief. We never understood just how dangerous it was. Francis was not taken to hospital, so he died at home and was buried three days after. I couldn't attend school while my favorite cousin was lying dead, and so I stayed home until he was buried.

When I eventually went back to school, Mr. Henry punished me for the absence. Before the punishment, he hit my head on the wall until blood started running down my back. I screamed and went home. When I arrived home, my mother was working in the garden and she just dropped everything and went with me to school just the way she was, with all the dirt on her hands and legs. Like a lioness whose cub had been hurt, she intended to attack and maul the teacher. It was the headmaster, Mr. Muzame, who managed to calm her down and prevent her from doing that. From that time, I was given a wide berth by teachers and bullies alike, and had an easier time at school, until it was time for me to sit for my eighth-grade national examination called the Kenya Preliminary Examination.

CHAPTER 5

A Step Ahead

My God is one step ahead of me with His mercy;
He will show me the victory I desire over my enemies.
—Psalm 59:10

It was a tradition in my time for high school students to get together at Christmas for parties. I had a distant uncle who had twelve children, most of whom were boys. The oldest were married girls, and their last-born girl was still too young. One of the boys, called Henry, went to school in Nairobi. During Christmas, he would borrow his older brother's record player for his high school students' parties. December of 1965 after I had just sat for my eighth-grade national examination, Henry came home with the record player from Nairobi. Normally, my mother would hear none of it, but this time she agreed that I should help serve Henry's visitors.

The party was held on Boxing Day, and I was there to help with the cooking and serving, alongside two other girls from the village. Beer was prohibited at these parties, but the food, soft drinks, and music were plenty. I was sixteen, and my body was developing. I shyly concentrated on my work, but there was this very good-looking boy, equally shy or perhaps just humble, looking at me. As the day wore on, he decided that looking wasn't enough. He started talking to me and helping me pass food. When I went to do the dishes, he was there helping me. My self-esteem had been lowered by the way Lily had brainwashed me into believing that I was ugly and undesirable, but that day in his presence, I felt different. The boy's name was Daniel, but his friends called him Dick (I know Americans use the name in unkind ways, but there it is). Personally, I called him Dan. He was going to eleventh grade, which we call form three. If I passed my exams, I was going to join form one, which put me two classes behind him.

By the time the party was over, we had clicked, and we had chemistry flowing between us. He was constantly on my mind long after he had gone back to Nairobi. He wrote me a long love letter, and I wrote back with all the vocabulary I studied from the dictionary. The letters never stopped and I wrote back. I told my mother about it. She was fine with it as long as the boy was far away. She used to give me thirty cents to buy a stamp every time I replied to Dan's letters.

Eventually, the results of the examination came and I had passed . . . with flying colors! After a long wait, I received an admission letter from Lugulu Girls High School. To merit a position in a government boarding school was very prestigious. My brother Jairus passed too and was admitted to Kenyatta College High School. Our adopted brother Elphas passed, but with a wife and a child, he had to be taken to his father's home to inherit his father's land. That's our culture; children belong to the father. I was heartbroken when he went, although the home was barely two miles away. He still came home on a regular basis, but he went to school in Nairobi and lived with his uncle. There was a culture of inviting church elders to pray for those who had worked hard to join high schools. The church people came to pray for me and my bother. Little did we know that they were burning with envy! We had made a lot of food. When the pastor stood to pray, he gave a long speech which left people baffled:

"We were here just a few years ago to pray for Dorcas, who went to Butere Girls High School. We haven't been to anybody else's house and here we are again," he continued. "Benson and his wives never went to school. How come every child of his passes examinations? Does it mean God resides in this home?"

At this juncture, my mother, the most outspoken of all, interrupted him. She told him not to pray and that we would pray by ourselves. She told the guests to sit and eat but not to worry about prayers. The occurrences of that day remained the talk of the village for a long time. It might as well have caused the end of inviting pastors to pray for students joining high schools because when my brother Laban joined Nyang'ori high school, my mother prayed herself.

There were only two buses that passed Lugulu on their way to Kitale. The Roadways bus passed very early in the morning. To get it, one had to be on the road at six o'clock. Missing it meant waiting for the OTC (Overseas Trading Company), a bus run by a British firm that passed at one o'clock. Missing that one meant trying the next day. Those going back to Kisumu had the same schedule. I did not know where the school was, so my father took me.

Lugulu School stood on a hill at the foot of Mount Elgon. It was proudly referred to by students as "The Green Hill Star," which was the name of the school magazine. Being at the foot of Mount Elgon, the place was as cold as Eldoret. With that kind of cold, students bathed outside with water that had been kept on basins under the beds overnight, which made the water colder.

The school had overgrown grass, and the grass served as a punishment for wrongdoers. They had to cut the grass with slashers or hoes. There weren't enough dormitories for all the students, so some classrooms were turned into dormitories. Each dormitory had a prefect called a "house mother." The house mothers behaved like real parents, yelling at students for no apparent reason other than to show their superiority and might. They wanted the students to respect them to the letter. I couldn't imagine comparing anybody else to my mother, whom I loved and respected deeply.

My abusive aunt had made me develop a thick skin. I respected house mother for a while, but when I saw that she was hard to please, I started defying her demeaning orders. I didn't really understand why Julia, my housemother, was so mean. We cleaned our dormitory, made our beds, and didn't carry food to the dormitory, but Julia still yelled. She made our lives a nightmare until some students thought it better to quit school. The headmistress, an American called Miss Bower, intervened and stripped Julia of her powers. We were so happy.

Miss Bower, the headmistress, wasn't the only American teacher we had. Most of the staff members were American Peace Corps volunteers. Kenya had just attained independence two years prior, and many nations of the world were coming in to assist us. Out of the twenty-eight teachers on the staff, only six were Kenyans. I had a hard time understanding their American accent, especially one older man who taught me Geometry and Algebra. His accent made me hate math just because I couldn't understand him.

A couple, Mike and Susan Stein, taught physics and biology respectively. I came to hate biology because Susan came to class with a chameleon. I have a phobia of the animal and so I would bolt out of the class every time she came in. I was punished several times in vain. I couldn't help it. Susan Orbeton made me love English. Miss Dillingham taught me literature, especially the book called *The Pearl*. As time went by, the Americans were phased out by the Kenyans. The best thing Americans did in that school was to ban beatings. Girls were only punished by being made to cut grass, but no beatings were instituted. Thanks to them, my beatings ended in eighth grade.

Although this school was government-run, it was also connected to the Quakers. The church had given out land for the construction of the school, and so there was a community church just beyond the school compound. This allowed the church to have a grip on the school. Sunday was a full church day. Students got up early to do their chores. We did all our house-keeping, but at least we had cooks. At eight o'clock, we went in for breakfast after which we attended Sunday school groups. At ten o'clock after Sunday school, we would have snacks, after which we headed straight to the community church. There was a narrow gate that we passed from the school compound to the church. The women's leader of that church came to stand at the church to inspect each and every girl, to see whether they had painted their nails or braided their hair.

According to the Quakers, it was sinful to wear nail polish, lipstick, earrings, or braids. As if that wasn't enough, the leader touched our bellies to find out if some of us were pregnant. In different places, in different times, that would definitely be considered harassment. I can assure you that girls didn't like that lady very much, but they had no way out. We didn't even understand the sermon, which was delivered in a different dialect, considering the fact that Lugulu Girls High School had students from all over the country, who spoke different languages. It didn't help that some of the students belonged to other faiths, like Islam. We were all expected to attend church under the watchful eye of Rasoa Mutua, the old lady who inspected us when we got to church. Most of us slept through the sermon.

After church, we had lunch at one o'clock. Sunday afternoon was free for those who received visitors. Nobody ever visited me in school—not even once—except after I cried, my father attended my last Parents' Day in that school. After dinner, we still had to go for night prayers, which ran from seven to nine. Basically, Sundays were God days.

Food was scarce. The portions were so small that we all adjusted our stomachs to that level. As little as our food was, we were the envy of other schools, whose food situations were even worse. We had beef and rice, which other schools did not. They only ate *ugali* (corn mash) with collard greens or kale. The most balanced diet of all was a mixture of corn and beans, with carrots and potatoes added.

I never had pocket money, but girls who came from wealthy families came with tons of money. If we didn't eat to our fill, they bought boiled corn, cassava or ripe bananas to subsidize the school's humble offering. Most of them were my friends, so even if I didn't have money of my own, I shared theirs. Saumu, Ruth, Mary, Tafroza, Rose, and Jessica were girls who had pocket money. I stuck with them, and they encouraged me to continue doing so. Some of them knew my home situation. Ruth was a sister-in-law to my sister. We were friends from the time we were in intermediate school because I used to stay with my sister during school holidays. My friends didn't ridicule me or laugh at my poverty. They simply loved me. When they bought cassava, sweet potatoes, or ripe bananas, we ate together.

By my second year in high school, I had become very open-minded and free to say anything I wished. I no longer cried for being bullied. In fact, I became the bully but not the beating type. I would scare the freshmen, but later on tell them it was meant to be a joke, all in an effort to strengthen them. They always ended up as my friends.

There were several social clubs in the school, and I think I joined most of them. I was a member of Christian Union, Debating Club, Drama, which was my favorite, and I even became a Sunday school teacher. This was mainly because we were allowed to go outside the school compound to teach in neighboring churches. The women of the particular church would give us food, a break from the monotonous school food. They gave us a little money as well.

Drama was my favorite because I memorized my lines very easily, and my acting talent was excellent. If I'd had a chance, like there are chances today, I would have made a career out of acting. We performed Shakespeare's *Merchant of Venice* so well that it took us on a tour around the country, acting in different schools. Apart from that, we acted other plays. If we needed men to play the male parts, we sometimes joined the neighboring Kamusinga Boys High School. We referred to the boys of that school as our "brothers across," as they called us "sisters across." I was a member of the school choir too. Choirs from the two schools joined when a mixed choir was needed to sing a particular song. I was also the best dancer in school especially on Saturday night when we had a record player for entertainment. The dancing made me a very popular figure on the campus.

Most teachers behaved like our parents or older brothers, unless a girl chose to entertain nonsense herself. We all respected each other responsibly as teachers and students, except one teacher who was posted to the school after his college degree and thought the girls were there for his taking. Some girls played along, as the teacher bragged that no woman could resist him. As he did his rounds with different girls, he sent one of them to tell me that he wanted to see me. I went to the office during night studies to see him. The teacher, who was called Clement, stretched his arms and got hold of me. Without him noticing, I wriggled myself out of my school jacket and left it in his arms. He didn't know what to do with it other than bringing it to me in class. He found me relating to other girls what had just happened and felt humiliated. From that time, I became his target. He would punish me unfairly, and he cited me on parade as the worst mannered girl on the school compound. Those who knew what was happening laughed out aloud though.

One evening when teacher Clement was on duty patrolling classes, he found some girls in my class talking ill of him. I was busy writing my English essay homework. He knew I wasn't part of the group that was discussing him, but he came after me with a cane stick to hit my head. The girls yelled at me to run for my life. I lifted my head, not knowing what was going on, and there Clement was, with a cane stick high up in the air, ready to strike. One of my friends Saumu, stood up to him from behind and caught up the stick in the air and pushed him so hard that he lost balance and fell to the ground. I ran out of the class and went to the dormitory, laughing at the drama when a group of girls surrounded me and told me to start crying and report it to the headmistress. They took me to her house and sure enough I was crying with bitter sobs. I tried to explain but I couldn't, so the girls took over the explanation, and told the headmistress what teacher Clement had been doing. She was very understanding but angry at the same time as to why the girls didn't report it earlier. The following day the board of Governors was called and Clement was transferred to a boys' school.

I wasn't a very good sportsperson, but I played netball, a girl's game similar to basketball. I played volleyball too and the two were my favorite sports. I also did some sort of high jump, but never athletics. I could never run. I felt as if my heart would burst if I tried to. I'd always had a problem with my heart, which went undiagnosed because there were no good hospitals and proper medical care then.

When I was younger, I would be playing outside the house one minute, and the next I would regain consciousness at the doctor's clinic, not knowing what had happened. There was only one private doctor who served the whole community, because my uncle Alpha lived far away from home, and only came once a month. His name was Mboku. It was Mboku who told my parents after listening to my heart with a stethoscope that there was a murmur in my heart. Then he gave me quinine because that was the only medicine he had for malaria and other ailments. I was later in life diagnosed with the same.

During my third year in high school, I fell ill and nearly died. Nobody was ever allowed to go home no matter how sick one was, but I was. Two girls from my dormitory had died, and I think the teachers didn't want another death on their hands. I went to the dispensary where an American nurse Sister Edith Ratcliff was in charge, several times but I didn't get better. I was allowed to go home. Within one week of the ailment, I had lost half of my weight. When I arrived home, walking like a zombie, M'ma just wept when she saw me. My mother had gone to the market, but word traveled very fast from the village. She came home, but her first worry was that I could be pregnant. Well, what she didn't know was that I feared to offend her by getting involved with boys. I was still intact. Several years later, I met Sister Ratcliff when I attended a Quaker Women's Conference in De Moines, Iowa in 1998. She had changed very little.

At the Lugulu dispensary, there was Dr. Boaz who still practices today, and Ezra, who's English we laughed at a lot. He used to ask us "where are you sickening?" when we went to the dispensary, which sounded very weird. It was understandable, but we laughed because he was an old man.

Do you remember Daniel, whom I called Dan? All this time, we never stopped communicating. He wrote letters every week and I wrote back. At first, they were friendly letters but later turned to love letters, with all the lies boys and girls tell each other. "I don't eat because you are too far away from me," he would write. I wrote back that I didn't breathe. I would only breathe when I saw him but it was definitely just figurative, to express love for each other; who can survive without eating or breathing for three years? I didn't even know him well; apart from the day he helped me serve food three years past. But I must say I yearned to see him because I had matured. An opportunity occurred in December of 1968. We were at our local church, practicing choral music for Christmas when he came to see me. He had long completed his high school and got a job with the Post Office Savings Bank.

The population of Kenya was only eight million people and human resources were needed. Recruiters for banks and other organizations used to visit schools and plead with the top students to work for them after they completed high school. This is how Daniel had gotten his job. Anyway, he had been given only two days to travel to the village for the burial of his sister, and was going back to Nairobi that same night. He had to see me, even if it was for five minutes. We talked for thirty minutes. I took him home for another few minutes, and then he took a night bus back to Nairobi. He said that he loved me and that he was not joking. He urged me to work hard in school so that our lives would be better. I knew he was indicating that he would marry me. I can assure you that that tape played in my mind for a long time. I said I loved him too, but it was another year and a half before I saw him again.

I loved my classwork, excelling in most subjects except biology and math for reasons I stated earlier. My hatred of domestic or home science continued from my intermediate days to high school. I couldn't bring myself to hold a needle to sew. The teacher, who came from Denmark, Miss Lenzing, didn't speak very good English, although she was a very nice person. She tried to make me like the subject in vain. Luckily a student had to take one compulsory science subject. An examination was set to judge which science class was best for each student. The first fifteen did physical science, the next thirty did general science, and the last group took health science. I found myself in the first fifteen. I was relieved to be among the big brains, as we called ourselves.

There were subjects I didn't consider subjects at all because they were just too simple for me. Those were English, Swahili, and Religious Education, which was all about Christianity, and having been raised in Sunday school on bible stories and rules, it was easy for me. The second easiest subjects were geography, history, and English literature. A problem came when I was forced to take compulsory subjects for my Cambridge Certificate of Education. These were math and biology, and I had to opt between Swahili and religious education, yet both were my favorites. I cried for three days, refusing to eat, becoming so dehydrated that I had to be rushed to the dispensary. After rehydration, I came back to school to be punished for having attempted suicide. Nobody understood my plight. I just knew that the teachers wanted me to fail my life-changing examination for reasons better known to them. I still did what the teachers wanted, despite having gone through hell. I had to drop religious education for Swahili.

The final year of high school was the best. The American headmistress had been replaced by a Kenyan woman called Salome Nolega David. This lady was among the first girls in my community to get a degree. Salome wasn't married, something unusual for girls of that time. The story was that she was hurt by a man and decided never to marry. She had a biological daughter and an adopted son. She was strong, assertive, and intimidating to those who expected to demean her on account of being a woman. The first thing she did was to change the way teachers dressed when they came to teach. Most of them wore flip flops. She said those were bathroom shoes. "You teachers are role models to these girls. What do you want them to learn from you?" she asked.

Male teachers started treating students with more respect. I must say that I developed such a liking for her that I just wanted to be like her—not because nursing and teacher were common options for females. Nursing was out of the question because my father would not have allowed me to. My uncle Alpha had told us that the final exam for a medical doctor was to spend a night in the mortuary with the dead, which my dad found bizarre and horrifying.

Salome made us develop very strong characters. We were no longer too shy to look a man straight in the eye and say no to his advances. I guess she had taken her disappointments as training grounds.

Salome taught us how to be ladylike, beginning with table manners, posture, dressing, and grooming. Most of all, she taught us how to dance to soul music, since that was the time James Brown was very hot with his soul music like "Baby, Baby, Baby, come on now!" It was a shift from our usual Swahili and vernacular songs, which had an African *Rhumba* and drum beat. She said she was preparing us to go into the world and compete with the rest of the people, and not just think of life around the village. I felt energized by her teachings, and I learned to be assertive as well, but only with people I already knew well. I still harbored the fear of strangers that had been instilled in me by my aunt during my early years of life.

If I could relive a segment of my life, I would choose my high school days. I was happy, free, and competitive. I had friends and foes alike. I was bullied and I bullied too. I enjoyed the clubs, especially choir and drama. And most of all, I enjoyed classwork because I was among the top students. Two things happened. While in form two, or tenth grade, I stood out as the best reader in class. My English teacher, a Kenyan called Hellen Omoka, just let me read page after page, while she and other students listened to me. At the same time, I was very good at story-telling, which made my essays very interesting.

While other students thought Hellen was just fond of me, and thus favoring me and rewarding me with one hundred percent points in essay writing, a student-teacher, Ahmed, relieved Hellen for some time. He too identified my talent in essay writing. He used to pin my essays on the school notice board for all to read. I became very popular in school, not because of my beauty, but because I was smart. It was after reading aloud a whole chapter in class that Hellen Omoka remarked "I will not be surprised to hear you read news on radio one of these days" she told me. Until that time, nobody knew how people got behind radios to talk through them. I had never heard of the career called journalism, and I didn't know what it took for one to be a broadcaster. At the time, it sounded as a joke. Very few homes had radios because many people couldn't afford them.

My uncle Samuel's boss gave him a radio but because he didn't want to pay the yearly license money of twenty shillings, he gave it to me, possibly to appease the way I was treated in his house. I must say that the radio became a tool for me to improve my English and Swahili spoken languages. But I didn't think I could ever be one of the broadcasters. Among my friends in intermediate school were two sisters whose parents were rich enough to own a radio. Other friends would make a point of converging in homes with radios to listen to music. We admired the broadcasters and assigned ourselves their names. It was a pleasant surprise when it happened that I would become a broadcaster.

Another thing happened during my high school days. I have already said that the school was at the foot of Mount Elgon and therefore very cold. Each student was given two blankets and two bedsheets when they first came to the school. Those beddings were to last the four years of high school. You took your beddings home after the four years. Some girls were from well-off homes and didn't want to take back the old blankets that they had used for four years, so they gave them to the remaining students.

During my third year of high school, there was a headmistress for just one semester called Miss Harrison. She took over from Miss Bower but after one semester, the board of governors could not stand her. That is when they brought in Salome Nolega. Miss Harrison would go around dormitory cubicles, and if she found any bed with more than one blanket, she assumed they had been stolen from other students. She accused me of such and I was not amused. She didn't want any explanations; her word was final. I tried to argue with her with an intention of making her understand the point, but she ended up suspending me from school for two weeks. The teachers and other students were sympathetic.

They told me not to go home, but make sure she didn't see me.

The teachers argued that they could not interfere with my studies when I was preparing for my final high school examinations. I therefore stayed in school, attended classes as usual, but went home the last weekend to get the tuition balance I had. She insisted that if I didn't pay the fees, she would not allow me back in school. I went home on Saturday and was back in her office on Monday. I paid the tuition and she told me that the onus was on me to catch up with the studies I missed. I just smiled politely. I had not missed anything because I had been in school all along. I will forever be grateful to my teachers and my fellow students who helped me keep watch out for the headmistress.

What worried me most was a bad report at the end of my school. So, nobody was happier than me at the beginning of the second semester, when school opened and Salome was the headmistress instead of Harrison. God must have heard my prayers.

CHAPTER 6

The Boyfriend

For God is not the author of confusion but of peace...
—1 Corinthians 14:33

The last day of high school was a memorable one. Our precious headmistress, Salome, wanted to introduce us to the world as girls. She hired a live band called Western Jazz Band to play music for us overnight. We were free to dance and even taste alcohol if one desired to. It was the first time I tried beer, and I didn't like it. I gave my bottle to my friend, Jessica. Since that time, I have been wondering why people crave beer, something bitter like medicine. I always took soda even when I was in the company of others, until somebody introduced me to wine. Even then, I can hardly drink more than one glass of wine. I later came to think about why I didn't like drinking at all, and concluded that I feared the wrath of my mother and God. This is an implicit psychological thought that cannot be explained. My mother raised me on biblical law, and the Sunday school shaped me to be a total believer. I'm glad I didn't get used to drinking. I had a hard task ahead of me which would not have gone hand in hand with drinking.

We dispersed the following day with some of us still drunk and others with hangovers. We had to be home early enough to vote because I was voting for the first time in my life. My candidate, James Onamu, made it to the parliament as my representative, the Honorable Member of Parliament for Hamisi Constituency, and came in handy. He was to help me achieve something I could not have done without his help.

I stated earlier that our fourth and eighth-grade examinations were national, but the examination taken in twelfth grade, or form four as we called it, was international. It was taken in East Africa, Kenya, Uganda, and Tanzania. The examination was set in Cambridge University, London. There were no computers, so the examination papers had to be airlifted physically to London for marking and grading. It was therefore a nerve-wracking period to wait for examination results to be announced from London, and that's why the names of candidates had to be printed in all the local dailies of the three countries. In our case, the results were delayed, prompting rumors that the airplane carrying the papers had burst into flames mid-air. Others made it even worse by suggesting that we were to repeat the examinations, and I couldn't bear that story. Results were announced on March 15, 1970.

The names of those who sat for this examination were published in the local dailies. If your name did not appear anywhere it meant that you had failed the examination. The results were classified in divisions. Division one was the highest, and the last was four. The less the points one had, the better the division. If one got eighty-five marks to one hundred percent, it was counted as an A, which was translated into a distinction with one point.

The subjects taken for that examination were a minimum of eight, with the best seven being counted towards the grade. One point was the best while the worst was nine points in every subject. I concentrated on my favorite subjects, ignoring biology and math, but because one of my worst subjects was counted, I failed to get a division one by one point. I was happy with a second division. After all, there were only two girls from my school in division one, three of us in division two, about twenty-eight in division three. I can't remember if we had any failures that year, but my race had been run, and the task was done. I was now free to jump and run.

Since I had emerged as one of the top students, having passed with a division two, I fitted into many slots and was therefore on very high demand everywhere. Salome wanted me to go back to school for two years and later go to the University for a degree in law. Kenyatta College offered Associate degrees for high school teachers, which we call diplomas in Kenya. I received an admission letter to join Kenyatta College. Moreover, there was a letter from Kericho Teacher Training College, for certification to teach in (primary) elementary schools. There was yet another letter requesting me to join Kenyatta Hospital to train in nursing.

All those training positions were sponsored by the government, and no fee was needed. But going back to school for a higher school certificate would have required me to pay tuition, which was hard to come by. Confusion took over. This was not to be the last time I'd vacillate over a decision. It was just the beginning. It is also the danger and predicament of students whose parents were illiterate and couldn't help them decide on a career. I was alone. I prayed, and then I came to a conclusion that I would go to Kenyatta College. I wanted to be like Salome, my high school headmistress, liberated, assertive, and confident.

Teaching in high school would also guarantee me a higher salary, and it would take a short time for me to start earning a salary to support my parents, especially my mother. She was illiterate but a matriarch who commanded respect in the home and in the village. It pained me to see her carry baskets of grain to market after market, day in day out, except Sunday, which was God's day. I wanted to relieve her so she could rest. I thought God had answered my prayer but that was not to be. A preacher once said that when one prays for something, the Devil rushes to get him or her counterfeit of whatever he or she wanted. I am sure that is what happened.

I had visited Nairobi a few times, to stay with my sister Selina and Truphena, who lived with their husbands, but my mother wasn't sure that I would arrive safely. She attached me to women she traded with—women who took fresh vegetables to Nairobi's markets twice a week, a distance of three hundred miles.

This time it was only Truphena, as Selina had moved to Kampala, Uganda, with her husband. I had also visited in August of 1967 during school holidays. That's when and where I saw Ugandan women kneeling down to serve their husbands with food and calling them "kings." I was horrified and wondered if those people never went to church to learn that you could only kneel before God and nobody else. I must have been seventeen, yet a Ugandan woman came to my sister's house to ask for my hand in marriage to her old husband! That was a man old enough to be my father. The women were so docile that they actually sought other wives for their husbands. During our time, it was not possible that a young girl befriended an older or married man, if the girl was educated. My sister went crazy, and I cried for a week, wondering if those people thought I was on sale. That was 1967, but in 1970, I was on my way to college so I could earn money to support my mother.

My sister picked me at the bus stop. I was at her house for three days before I went to college.

Kenyatta College was a former army barracks that had been transformed into a national high school on one side and a teachers' college on the other side. There were only three hostels for women, named after East African Mountains. One was Longonot, another was Ruwenzori, and the last was Suswa. The male halls were as far as a mile away, and they had to walk to college every morning and back. I was given a room in Suswa. My room-mates were Susan and Norah, but Norah was my closest friend. She was a tall and heavily built, and very sweet-natured. When we walked together, one would think it was mother and daughter. I used to take her to Daniel's house, hoping she would get a boyfriend from there, but she didn't. She had just lost her boyfriend, a married man and member of parliament for her area, in a car crush. I came to know her when she was still recovering from the loss and often crying. Apart from the ladies, I found myself hanging out with a group of men from my area too. Those people were comedians, and they made me laugh, until one of them tried to turn the true friendship into a love affair and I promptly quit their group.

Dining services were cafeteria style, using tickets we were issued every month. There was no way you could use a ticket from another month because each month had a different color of tickets. Because the college was government sponsored, students ate like kings: bacon, sausages and eggs for breakfast; rice, chapatti and other healthy foods for lunch and dinner.

The classes I took were English, Swahili, and history. Both Swahili and English were divided into two parts: literature and language. I loved English and history, but the Swahili we learned was more like Arabic than Swahili as I knew it. The Swahili lecturer was actually an old Arab called Albusaidy. For the first time, I started loathing the idea of going to a Swahili class. I found it hard to construct one sentence of "Mashairi" or Swahili poems. I loved English linguistics and literature, in which we learned how to read fast using a gadget called Rapid Reader. It was amazing.

Meanwhile, I had written a letter to Daniel to tell him I was coming to Nairobi. He knew my sister, and he knew her house in Makongeni, an estate for railway workers. Makongeni was built in such a way that four blocks, comprising ten living units, making a total of forty houses, shared two bathrooms and two toilets for women and the same number for men. People who could not wait for their turns just did it outside, around the toilet block. The whole estate stunk. Many residents improvised bathrooms on their verandas, but they still had to visit the dirty bathrooms for number two. I didn't like what I saw, but I couldn't tell my sister because Africans are euphemistic. We go around a topic, avoiding calling a spade a spade and not a big spoon. My brother-in-law, Manase, a technician with East African

Railways and Harbors, merited the large houses the company provided in an upper-class estate, but because the house would take more money from his pay check, he opted for the single-roomed houses. He always saved money for his children's school fees.

A family could raise ten children in that single room, with most of them sleeping under the father and mother's bed, of course. It was therefore a welcome idea to see Daniel with my cousin Henry coming to see me. This was the third time I was seeing him. I was a bit more mature than I had been the first two times. I was educated, and I could reason and take part in a conversation. But love has another language that comes with shyness, and even the strong can be overpowered. Dan took me to his house and brought me back after two hours.

The second time I stayed longer, and the third and fourth time, and then I spent a night. My brother-in-law was so mad that he took it out on my sister. They fought over my going to my boyfriend's house. I had long joined Kenyatta College and therefore decided to boycott my sister's house, instead going straight to Daniel's house. I made it a habit of never spending the weekends on the college compound. If I did, Daniel would come for me, and love at that time made the world go round. There was another reason why I could not spend weekends on the college compound. College life seemed to revolve around who was sleeping with whom, something I could not bring myself to discuss. The older students were always in wait for freshmen so as to make their pick. In my case, there was a second-year student called Moses.

Moses wanted to literally force his love on me. I could not reciprocate his feelings for me because my heart was elsewhere. He became violent when I told him I had another boyfriend. I didn't know that the ways of Nairobi dictated people to have more than one boyfriend and girlfriend. I remember him telling me that I would be disappointed one day, and that I shouldn't run to him when it happened. Why would I be disappointed? I was in love with Daniel and I wholly trusted him. I believed he loved me too.

Then a time came when students rioted at Kenyatta College and the anti-riot police were called in. They beat up students and arrested some of them. Two of our colleagues died in the melee as scores were injured. I was so terrified that I took and sought refuge in Daniel's house for a few days, after which Grace came to the house and found me.

Grace was an older girl who was already working. I did not even suspect that she could have had anything going with Daniel. Every time Grace came to the house, Daniel took my hand and led me out of the house. We went to town or just strolled around, talking. Daniel lived with two other young men, Japheth and Evans. I always thought that Grace came to see one of the other men. Never did it cross my mind that she was the other woman in Daniel's life. She was better dressed because she had a job and could afford anything for herself. I never had new clothes. All I had were hand-me-downs from my sisters, obviously oversized, because I was very slim.

Grace was short, busty, and voluptuous—what the young ones would call "bootilicious" nowadays. She always wanted people to discuss office matters, knowing that I could not contribute because I was a mere student. Still, I did not see it. I continued coming to Daniel's house, sometimes meeting Grace there, and sometimes not, because she had her own apartment. In fact, there was a day Daniel was attacked by thugs at night as he walked from Grace's house and hospitalized for two days. The thugs tried to choke him, and as he screamed for help, he hurt his vocal cords. He told me a different story, but I later came to know the truth. The truth came when Daniel took me to hospital. I had been sick with abdominal pains for a week and when a pregnancy test was done, it came out positive.

The news was as unexpected as it was shocking. The first person I thought about was my mother. I was worried that I had disappointed her. I looked at Daniel and did not see the excitement of a person who had just received the news that he was going to be a father. Then I remembered what Moses had told me: that I would be disappointed. How had he known? Maybe Daniel was just worried that I was sick and pregnant, and that I was going to mess up my education. Daniel was a happy man, always laughing and making others laugh, but this changed after we saw the doctor. He became subdued and unusually silent.

Back in college, I continued to be sick. I threw up at the sight of anything I did not like. I could not eat. I carried handkerchiefs into which I spat because my mouth was always full of saliva which I could not swallow. We were given a bar of soap by the college for bathing. I hated the brand, and to this day, I cannot stand that soap, almost fifty years down the line. The water was warm and nice, but I couldn't take any showers. Everything had a bad smell, including the air around the college. I quit college, leaving everything behind. I went to Daniel's house and found Grace as the woman of the house. She hissed when she saw me, but I didn't say or do anything. I waited for Daniel to come home from work. As soon as he entered through the door, Grace met him, kissing him and taking the package he was carrying. She reminded me of the Ugandan women. Daniel didn't even greet me. He went to the bathroom, took a shower came back, and asked me to go out with him. I thought we would take our usual stroll, but he took me to the bus stop and told me to go and never come back to mess up his life because he was now married to Grace. I simply asked him, "Are you sure?" When he answered, "Yes," I couldn't believe my ears. How foolish could I be? How blind was I? I hated myself, but then I remembered Salome David and all her teachings. "Do not let any man look down upon you," she would say.

I thought about Moses and how he told me that I would be disappointed. I looked Daniel in the eye and told him I was going and would never come back to beg him, but he would be the one to beg. Without turning back, I walked away and raised my hand to flag down a bus which was approaching. It stopped, and only when I sat down did I turn back to see Daniel still standing where I had left him, face down to the ground. The bus took a turn at a corner as it headed to town. I felt nauseated. I took a seat, opened the window, and puked.

When I arrived in town, I alighted from the bus and took another bus from town to Makongeni. That was the only place I could go, and this time I was willing to ignore the stench. My sister was welcoming, but she noticed there was something different about me. There was no way I could hide it. I simply blurted it out that I was pregnant, and that Daniel, the nice boy who everybody knew and respected, had dumped me. I found her reaction funny because the first thing that came from her mouth was, "Abortion."

I had sworn to God while in school that if I ever got pregnant out of wedlock and tried to abort, that God should take me in the process. I still remembered it vividly. I had also seen girls in high school get pregnant, and when they tried to abort, they died. The reason is that abortion was, and still is illegal in Kenya. Girls procured abortions through dubious means, assisted by quacks. While some died in process, others were left sterile, not being able to have children forevermore. There were many barren women whom I knew that wished they could just get pregnant for a day. I wasn't going to be one of them. My religious upbringing also contributed to my belief that every child had a right to live, and that God knew how the child would grow.

There is a saying in my mother tongue that goes like this: "Every baby comes with its package." If the birds of the air can eat, what of a human being with two hands! I decided to keep my baby. My sister wasn't the only one who tried to convince me to have an abortion, however. Many people, including men, thought that I should not forfeit my education because of a baby. I reasoned that I could get education anytime, but I didn't know if I would get another baby. I didn't think of the baby in terms of the father who had snubbed me. I wanted to hold my baby in my arms.

My brother-in-law had been paying his sister's fees to study in high school and subsequently for teacher training college. My sister wanted him to help me too, but he refused. Even so, I can understand that they may not have had enough money. There was a tug-of-war between my sister and her husband. It was unfortunate that his sister failed her examination while I passed highly. My sister talked sarcastically about it. Now, me getting pregnant and dropping out of school had just given my brother-in-law a weapon against my sister. Every evening after work he would come home and start the story of stupid children who wasted their parents' money on education, then got pregnant. When I got tired of hearing the same song over and over, I just left the house and didn't go back. I went home to the village, but life in the village was worse. My mother lamented every day, weeping exactly as if I was dead. Her lamenting went along lines like:

"I thought I was going to stop carrying baskets. I hoped my time to rest had come. Why did I waste my money? You should have died young like my other children. Why did you survive to make me a laughing-stock?"

She would cry all through the night and any time she saw me during the day. The villagers even added fuel to the fire by saying that they could never waste money educating girls. Boys take care of parents and homes. High school girls started avoiding me like I was contagious. I had no friends in the village. I became a total pariah. The church didn't spare me either. They stripped me of my youth leadership roles and asked me to stay away from the church. I had committed a sin.

I got so tired of the whole situation that I left home without telling anybody where I was going. I took a bus and went to Nakuru, one of the largest cities in Kenya. I had lived there with my uncle Samuel and his family, when I used to visit them during school holidays. The irony is that even if I escaped Lily's torture, I still visited during school holidays. I was too old to be verbally abused. We had moved from

Eldoret to Kericho, then Nakuru, after a short stint in Athi River. In Nakuru I became friends with a girl called Florence.

Then, my uncle and aunt moved to Kabete in Nairobi, and Florence took me in. She worked at a gas station and had a very tiny apartment. She was the only one I could think of at that juncture. We shared her bed and everything. Her salary wasn't enough to support both of us, so she had a sugar daddy, a member of parliament, and an older man who later married her as a third wife. The man used to do our grocery shopping to make life bearable. Meanwhile, I was looking for a job. I was interviewed at Barclays Bank. I passed all the interviews but failed the medical examination because I was pregnant. It was the norm for companies to reject pregnant women, even when they were married. If it happened to me now, I would sue them, but the legislation then actually allowed it. I was four months pregnant at the time, although it didn't show much, and it was during one of my job-hunting sprees that I met a man from my village called Elijah.

Elijah was shocked to see me. Apparently, people in the village had been mourning my death since I left home. Communication wasn't easy, and I didn't tell anybody before leaving home. Nobody would have thought I would be in Nakuru because the uncle I used to visit had since moved to Nairobi. Elijah said that the villagers were ridiculing my mother for driving me to my death. Listening to all those stories made me compassionate about my mother. I decided to go back home. My mother was happy to see me, and for a change, she treated me with respect. She became my friend who told me that it was not the end of the world. She became supportive, and I felt that I belonged.

A month after I went home to the village, I got a reprieve when Beatrice and Jane came home to the village, pregnant as well. They had both been to Kaimosi Girls High School. Jane had graduated high school, but Beatrice was a third-year high school student when she got pregnant. We became the inseparable trio. At least when we met and talked, we could even laugh about the way people were treating us. Jane was the first, getting twin girls, but one died. Beatrice was second with a son, and I had my own son on March 15 of 1971, exactly one year after I received the results of my Cambridge certificate. A lot had happened during that one year.

With my son born, I quickly sunk back into poverty, more than ever before. The poverty was visible during pregnancy. I didn't have any maternity dresses. I had no money to shop for my baby. The father had denied me, and the people in the village couldn't stop pointing fingers at me. They would pretend to greet me politely but after I passed, I would turn back instinctively only to find them staring at me. One woman spat at me saying, "These are the ones who speak English," which meant that I had wasted money going to school only to get pregnant. My life was a nightmare, but since my mother treated me with a little respect, I felt that was what mattered most.

It so happened that Judith, my cousin, who was Lily's firstborn was pregnant too. She was defiled by an old man who worked with my uncle. She had a baby girl, but the baby died after one month. Rumors had it that Judith had accidentally crushed the baby in its sleep, but that's where it ended—as a rumor. If Judith had not been pregnant, Lily would have been the main trumpet player in the village, informing people about my pregnancy. God knows how to stop malice.

CHAPTER 7

Face to Face

Behold I am doing a new thing!
Now it springs up; do you not perceive it?
I am making a way in the desert, and
streams in the wilderness . . .
—Isaiah 43:19.

When I was still a student at Tigoi Intermediate School, there was a need to upgrade it to high school status. Those kinds of schools were called secondary schools, and they were run by the community. Tigoi was therefore upgraded into a secondary school in 1963, making it primary, intermediate, and secondary. Many students who would have otherwise missed high school education in government school had a chance. Most of them came from the same community. Such schools suffered lack of teachers, which affected enrollment. Moreover, they only went up to form two, and then students would sit for the Kenya Junior Secondary School Examination.

Those who passed with good marks could join a government high school in form three. Tigoi was no exception. The board of governors made use of interdicted teachers in the community, or those laid off in the public interest for lack of discipline or drunkenness. Such teachers could be paid peanuts. Tigoi suffered as well, and by January of 1971 was the only teacher who drank too much during class hours. After some students helped to carry him home, they dispersed and never came back to school. The parents weren't about to make the biggest mistake of their lives, paying a drunk their hard-earned money. The board therefore came to my home to plead with me to stand in while I was still awaiting delivery of my baby. They were very careful not to mention my pregnancy. I didn't remind them of how everybody thought I was a loser, before thinking I could help.

The first day I went to class, there were only four students in the whole school. They religiously reported to school every morning, hoping a teacher might appear. When I stepped into the class, heavily pregnant, the students applauded and gave me a standing ovation even before they knew I had come to teach them. Those four students played a very important role of advertisement by word of mouth. By the end of the week, I had sixteen students, and twenty-eight in two weeks' time. They said that they had heard there was a very good teacher. I hoped I wouldn't disappoint them.

My biggest problem was that there were no books, nor was there a library. I started soliciting books from neighboring schools, and anybody who had textbooks they didn't need donated. Another problem was that I hated biology and math, and I had to have somebody who wasn't a drunk to teach those subjects. Fortunately, an old boy of

Tigoi Intermediate, my former classmate, was in the village doing nothing. I brought him aboard. There was another boy who had completed his higher school certificate but didn't pass well enough to join any university. I employed him too. Now, we were three teachers with one class of twenty-eight students. We worked hand in hand, and the students were hungry for education. I was heavily pregnant by then. On March 12, 1971, I started having signs of labor. They gradually increased without me knowing what they were.

I labored for four days before finally delivering my baby. I didn't know what to expect, and so I thought it was normal to have such prolonged labor. There was no money for hospitalization, and the hospitals were very scarce. Village women were in attendance. The fourth day, at seven o'clock in the evening, my son was born. I passed out immediately afterward out of sheer fatigue and dehydration because I hadn't been eating for the four days. It took me three hours to come around, only to find people crying that I had died. They had already sent word to all relatives to come home for my funeral, but God was on my side. He wanted me to live and raise my son.

I didn't have money to buy new baby clothes or anything, but my old bath towel that I used at school came in handy. My son was naked for two weeks for lack of clothes. I had to rip my old clothes into pieces to make little outfits by hand. I regretted that I hadn't taken to domestic science in school. That would have enabled me to stitch better clothes. I know some people will ask what I did with the money I earned as a teacher at Tigoi Secondary School. The answer to that is that we were not salaried. It was like doing community voluntary work. The little stipend we were given once in a while was not enough. Believe me or not, I saved mine to buy iron sheets so I could build my father and mother a decent house. Decent means that it could have mud walls and dusty floors, but it should have had a corrugated iron sheets roof. That I did with the help of my brother-in-law Japheth, husband to Selina.

I was lucky that the labor lasted only through the weekend and by Monday I had my son, who I named Victor, for I wanted him to conquer the world. I prayed that he would become a winner in life because he was born in adversity. I was in class teaching by the following Monday, after a week's rest. I was determined to help my community—a community that had looked down on me for getting pregnant. I wanted them to see that it was not the end but the beginning of my life. I wanted them to see that it is possible to leave vengeance unto God. I wanted to preach that it was possible to rise above your adversity and move on; that harboring animosity just hurts yourself.

My community is patriarchal, and children belong to the father. This means that in the case of a divorce, which was almost nonexistent then, the children remain with the father's side. If the father died and the mother wanted to remarry she would leave the children behind to be raised by paternal grandparents. It also means that the naming of babies is done by a paternal grandfather or paternal grandmother in the absence of the former. I had delivered a baby in my parents' house, a baby whose father didn't care about. I decided to see what would happen if I kept him and if I named him by myself. That's why I named my baby Victor, although I also called him Felix, a name I liked from my school days. When I took him for baptism at the Tigoi Friends Church, the elders chose the name Felix, but inside, I knew he was a Victor. My mother had to hold the baby during baptism because I was still a sinner, but my son was not. That was fine with me.

For the first month, Victor cried non-stop. Now I know it was colic, but my clan claimed that the baby needed his clan name, which could only be given by his grandfather. I was willing to do anything for my son. I had a love for him that I had never known that existed between human beings. It makes me understand the love of God for human beings, his children.

Owing to the fact that my son cried a lot, supposedly for a name, I made the decision to take him to his paternal ancestry home for a naming ceremony. It was during Easter holiday, which are celebrated in Kenya by being off work on Good Fridays and Easter Mondays. I took part of my savings to build a house for my parents and hired a vehicle to take me to Hamisi. In the company of my mother and my cousin's wife, we arrived there at eight o'clock in the morning. People in the home were woken up by the racing of the car. Apart from the naming ceremony, the baby's paternal grandmother was to shave his first hair, especially for the first child. That side of the family was also supposed to have bought the first baby blanket, soap, and powder. It is a general belief that if people did those things for a child that did not have their blood relation, the child dies. It is therefore a way of proving that the baby is theirs.

As fate would have it, Daniel was at home, having come to the village for his Easter holidays. His brother Zack was there too, plus his two sisters. Daniel's father, Jacob, a tall strong man, carried all the excitement of the day. We were ushered into the parents' house as Jacob took charge, summoning everybody to make haste in whatever they were doing. After serving us tea with bread, we stated the nature of our mission. Jacob took the baby from my hands and lifted him up to God, both physically and in prayer. He blessed the baby and gave him endless names belonging to his dead relatives. Some names were very long, like Mudengeya, Mujivane, Kijereji but I picked the shortest so I could remember it. That was Lidaywa.

My mother-in-law shaved the baby clean as Daniel and his brother Zack rushed to the shopping center to buy a small baby blanket and some clothes. This was the first time I had seen Daniel since we parted at a bus stop in Nairobi when I was pregnant. He looked at his son and saw that he was a copy right of his grandfather, whose looks Daniel had too. He smiled and held him. Grace in Nairobi had failed to conceive, yet here was his own blood son living in abject poverty. He didn't say anything, but I thought I saw something in his eyes. Everybody wanted me to stay, but I wouldn't hear any of that. Our mission had been accomplished, and we had no business hanging around. We left. The total time we spent in the home was two hours. Salome's teachings were still rife in my ears. "Nobody owns life except the Creator," she would say. I knew Daniel may have had money, but he didn't own my life or the life of our son.

I am not just being superstitious when I say that the baby stopped crying after a visit to his grandparents' home. Somehow it worked. My baby became so sweet that you couldn't tell he was the same one who cried all the time. I made a plan with the other teachers to be at school earlier, so that I made sure the baby was comfortable before I left for school. I fed him and gave him a bath in the morning. He slept until I came home for lunch. He was awake for as long as I ate my lunch and fed him, then he went back to sleep. I came back home from work at four-thirty, and he would just be getting up. That was his sleep pattern for a long time.

CHAPTER 8

Respect

I have seen something else under the sun:
The race is not to the swift, nor the battle to the strong,
nor does food come to the wise, or
wealth to the brilliant,
or favor to the learned; but time and
chance happen to them all . . .
—*Ecclesiastes 9:11*

Tigoi secondary school flourished because I decided to make it a girls' school and it had to be a boarding. For a long time, education revolved exclusively around males. There were many boys' high schools around us, like Nyang'ori, Vihiga, and Chavakali. The only girls' school in Hamisi was Kaimosi. The board welcomed my idea and together we started to find ways and means of accommodating the female students, while the boys would remain day scholars, and would be phased out. I made an appointment with honorable James Onamu, the Member of Parliament for Hamisi Constituency and told him what I was planning to do. He came in to support the projects by fundraising and soliciting for books. He knew the project would earn him respect and votes when the time came, and it sure did!

The community had started viewing me with respect. They started arguing that it was just a natural accident that I got pregnant prematurely. Some men were referring to me as their "brother" and not sister, as Africans refer to each other, because they said I had the brain of a man. Men were still respected and given the first priority. If there were two students in a family, and the parents could only afford tuition for one of them, even if the girl was smarter, the boy would be the one to get an education. That's how bad it was. Therefore, for me to be recognized as having brains like that of men was a big honor. Whatever I suggested, the board agreed with me, so it was easy when I suggested that we put out an appeal for anybody who had an extra bed or beddings to donate to the school. We got more than enough. I identified a building that used to be a workshop for former students who learned carpentry, remodeled it, and turned it into a dormitory. Twenty-two students started living at school. Six students were boys who remained day scholars and were phased out gradually.

I doubled as a teacher and headteacher, and sometimes also acted as the matron, making sure the boarding students were comfortable and had enough food. In November of that same year, 1971, I saw Daniel coming to see me at school. I was very casual and civil about the whole situation. I allowed him into the office and waited to hear what he had to say. He said he had three things on his mind. One, he came to tell me to take his son to his home for baptism. They belonged to the Pentecostal Assemblies of God Church, while we were

Quakers, a religion that my illiterate mother believed was the mother of all religions in the world. Nobody could convince her otherwise. Remember, my son had been baptized in my church, and now the paternal grandparents insisted that the baby had to be baptized in their own church.

Two, he had come to inform me that his sister Flora would be wedding and that I had to attend, apart from taking the baby to his auntie's wedding, although he was only eight months old. And three, he said he was tired of living far away from his son, with a woman who couldn't understand right from left. I knew that was a trick many men used to deceive women that they were more special than the one in the house. I simply told him that Grace was the woman of his choice, to which he replied, "Not anymore." Without me asking how and why, he went on to explain that Grace had been told that I took the baby to his father's home and that Daniel was there. She complained that Daniel shouldn't have bought anything for the boy without asking her. The verbal fight accelerated, and ended up with Grace carrying everything from Daniel's house, including his underwear, and going to an undisclosed destination. Word had it that she had been transferred to a different town for work. He didn't even hide the fact that his friends, especially one called Sonny, with whom he'd gone to school, had shunned him for being manipulated by a woman to ignore his own son to suffer in the village.

As he spoke those words, I saw a type of vulnerability in him that I had never seen. Tears ran freely down his face. "I have therefore come to ask for your hand in marriage so we can raise our son together as a family" he concluded. "I am sorry for what I put you and the baby through" he said.

Tears gripped me. I had always known that men only cry when things are very bad. I only saw my father cry twice; when his sister, Freda died, and much later when my brother Jairus died.

The idea of going down on bended knee for a proposal is foreign to most Africans. I told him how he had embarrassed me, humiliated me, cost me my teacher training, and left me suffer with the baby. I had made a decision to remain like Salome; never to get married but raise my son on my own. My parents, as other community members were not amused as it was unheard of for a woman to refuse marriage. Before that, many people had come to ask me to marry them, or marry their relatives but I wasn't walking into the trap of men again. I'd played with fire and burned my hands once. Daniel had been my first, but he disappointed me. I wasn't about to allow that to happen to me again. They always say that once beaten, twice shy. I said I had to think about the whole thing, but I would take the boy for another baptism, and that I would attend Flora's wedding because she was my friend. Flora was marrying Japheth, a friend of Daniel's and a distant cousin to me.

In early December, 1971, I took the baby to Hamisi, and the pastor doing the dedication couldn't pronounce the name Felix, so he picked Victor. His father was also very happy with the name Victor because it belonged to a character in a comic magazine that every youth during our time read. It was very popular and the main character Victor was like the 'Superman' of the time. The character always won impossible battles. Nearly everybody who was a teenager at that time has a son called Victor. My parents, my sisters and brothers, my uncles, and my cousins had all urged me to listen to the father of my child. There was no point in me struggling to raise him alone as a single parent when the father was very much willing to marry me. The deal was then sealed when I went back to Hamisi mid-December for the wedding.

My own wedding had been set for January and it would take place in Nairobi. After Flora's wedding, I too went to Nairobi. The wedding between me and Daniel was held on January 8, 1972. I had to hurry back home to school for form one recruitment exercise. We had fifty-six form one students crammed into one class, until we decided to make it a double stream. Unfortunately, I had just entered into a contract with someone who would dictate my life again.

Daniel said that he had married me to live with him in Nairobi and raise our son together. I needed to go to Nairobi and take a different course, which would enable me to live at home. I had to abandon the school I had come to love so much. My students cried when I said I was leaving. Honorable James attended the farewell party and heaped praises on me. Even the traditional old men in the community who had been opposed to my heading the school, claiming that it was a job for their sons, were affected by my leaving. Emotions ran high at the farewell party, as the school girls wailed uncontrollably. I too shed tears.

Before I left, I advertised my position and the board and I picked Peter, who came from a different constituency. One thing the community loved me for was that I had created jobs for people who would otherwise have languished in drinking moonshine. The cooks, the cleaners, those who worked in construction, and produce suppliers all came from the community. Apart from that, businesses at Tigoi shopping center was booming for those who sold pens, ink, girls' underwear, and those who boiled corn, sweet potatoes, and cassava to sell to students over the fence, benefited a lot. The economy of the area improved as people took their children to school while others built better housing than what they had before.

Honorable James could be heard in public meetings bragging as to how he had improved the status of the area. This earned him votes for a second term in the parliament, and everybody was happy. When I left and Peter took over, he fired everybody I had employed and brought in his own people from his area. There was an outcry, but Peter didn't care. Because I loved the school, I always wanted to know the progress. When I visited the village, I would go to check on the school, but Peter wouldn't even want to see me. There was an uproar and protests. While in Nairobi, I met James and asked him to help the school be taken over by the government. He did, and an American Peace Corp volunteer was brought in to head the school instead of Peter. As I write this book, the school is one of those government schools that perform very well, both academically and in sports. During the first few years after I left, my name was mentioned in parents' meetings as the founder of the school. Somebody must have decided to blot me out. Secondly, I am nominated to serve on several school boards, like Masana, Vihiga, Gimarakwa, and Chepkebuge, but never have I been proposed by Tigoi. I believe in the saying that only God rewards wholeheartedly.

My shortcomings had made me accomplish something I had never dreamt of doing. If I hadn't gotten pregnant in college, there may never have been a girls' high school in Tigoi. Romans 8:28 reads, *"And we know that in all things*

God works for the good of those who love him, and who have been called according to his purpose."

When I read other people's testimonies, I often compare them with my story. I should think you, as my reader, is doing the same. Whatever you are facing right now, believe that God knows why and that something good and positive will come out of your present conditions. I have since learned to say, "Never give up."

CHAPTER 9

Marriage and Life

*Love bears all things, believes all things,
hopes all things, endures all things.*
—*1 Corinthians 13:7*

Life with Daniel in Nairobi was generally good. He was soft-spoken and peace-loving, but he loved discipline. He disciplined Victor by spanking him, something I did not like. I loved my son so very much. Anybody touching him may as well have touched me directly. We often argued about the spanking, but he insisted that a child must learn to be responsible at an early age. I started questioning the decision I had made to marry Daniel. The fact that he rejected me while pregnant resulted in him not bonding with the baby from birth. I felt it was not his duty to spank my son, although he was the father. I thought he didn't love him, but I later came to discover that he was the best father in the world, although he may not have been a perfect husband the way I would have wanted him to be.

We lived in Pangani area of Nairobi, near Mlango-Kubwa, a Swahili name meaning the Big Door. I have always why the estate bore that name despite having neither a big door nor gate. The apartment was one large room, which served both as living room and bedroom partitioned by curtains. The kitchen served as a house help bedroom and cooking place. You may be wondering why we had help. In Kenya, the working hours with most jobs, including schools, are eight to five. If you have to keep a job and juggle it with family, you must live with somebody to take care of your children while you work. It also helps the house help to earn a little money to send home to support their poor parents. Daniel was already working, but I needed a job, or at least to go to college. But first I had to be sure that Daniel was true to his word about marriage.

Daniel was hardly at home. He worked every day of his life. There were opportunities at his workplace for overtime, and he grabbed the chances and worked three extra hours every weekday and worked ten overtime hours on Saturday and Sunday. At first, I didn't understand why he wouldn't rest even on a weekend, but I came to realize that he had an urge to shake off the poverty he had grown up in and make a difference in his life. I was good with it. We had everything we needed, and his son was always well and expensively dressed, even though I wasn't.

I didn't know how and why he never realized that I had to dress properly, but I never asked him nor did I complain. By the end of March that year, I became seriously ill, throwing up all the time and not eating anything. I was pregnant again. This meant that I couldn't work or go to college. I stayed home, dealing with my pregnancy.

By the time I was six months pregnant, my sister-in-law Tabitha came to visit. She stayed with us for two weeks. Tabitha was a greedy person who thought everything in her brother's house must belong to her as well. She ransacked the house, taking almost everything we had, including a radio, cooking pans, cutlery, and some of my clothes. My husband let her take them, saying "we will get more," which I didn't like at all. I thought he was being too weak to face his sister. Then he did the unthinkable of dispatching me to the village with his sister and my son Victor.

I need to tell non-Kenyan readers to realize that in Africa, people have two homes. The ancestral home is in the country, while people flock to urban centers in search of employment, making them establish another home in town. Most people live far away in towns where they work while the family lives in the village. Daniel had put up a semi-permanent house in which I lived, next to his parents' house. Tradition demands that until a wife is officially declared independent, she cooks and eats with the family. This meant that I could only eat when others ate. My son would cry with hunger, but I didn't have anything to do. My sister-in-law Jessica had five children in the home, from four different fathers.

My mother-in-law seemed to favor those children. I may be wrong, but that was my observation. I never had money to spend on food because Daniel knew his parents were in charge of buying food. My child and I were just passengers on the family bus, although my mother-in-law would once in a while insist that I go to the farm and plant potatoes, heavily pregnant as I was. I could hardly bend, but because in Africa we are socialized to respect the elders, I tried to do as she wanted. She was generally a nice woman, soft-spoken, short, and quite beautiful. Daniel took most of her features, the stature, the brown skin, the curly hair, and beautiful eyes. His father Jacob was very tall, dark, and strong, but must have been handsome as a young man. His only flaw was that he was loud and quarrelsome, yelling at everybody all the time. He was never on the same side of a discussion with anyone. If he argued with someone about something, he opposed the other person. If the person changed his mind to support his views, Jacob would change his mind and still oppose the other person. This made people hate or fear him. He had no friends and never listened to any advice.

I was full of regrets. I wondered why I had left my teaching job at Tigoi to live with a husband, who has sent me to the village to live with his parents. My freedom of feeding my son any time I wanted was curtailed. I lived a lonely life like I wasn't married. I was brilliant in school and deserved to have a job but not remain a stay-at-home mother. I was full of envy in seeing people I'd gone to school with but failed their examinations earning their own money while I was still like a beggar, depending on a man who didn't seem to care. Daniel himself was not a friend of his father at all. I don't know why he expected me to get along with him.

My second son was born on November 18, 1972. My mother who lived eleven miles away had a dream that I had delivered a baby boy. She sent my cousin Joyce, whom my mother adopted with some money and foodstuff. She found me in labor, but I didn't tell her; Africans do not discuss labor with other people. I didn't even tell my mother-in-law, who forced me to plant sweet potatoes with her. I told her that I forgot to take my medicine and that I had a headache. I walked to the house, took a bath, and headed to the nearest dispensary, which could be seen over the fence from our home.

My father-in-law, who was herding cows on the dispensary compound, saw me and knew I was in labor. He took charge, holding my hand and leading me to an office and then left me to look for the nurse. He brought in the nurse and yelled at her to give me a bed, as I was in pain. He frantically rushed home to yell at my mother-in-law, asking why she had let me walk to the dispensary alone. My mother-in-law tried to hurry to the dispensary but it started raining heavily and continued for two hours. But Salome, the wife of my brother-in-law, was with me. She had seen me walk out of the compound and knew what was going on. By the time my mother-in-law came after the rain stopped, I had delivered a nine-pound baby boy. My mother-in-law was given a bed to spend the night with me in the ward because I was the only patient. It was rare for women to deliver babies at a clinic. They always did it at home for fear of being branded a coward. I couldn't have cared less.

I named my son Felix, the name I had carried forward from Victor, but that was not to be. My sister-in-law, Flora, whose wedding I went to attend, came home sick. She was married for one year in which she had had three miscarriages. Flora wanted a baby with all her heart. She said to me "Mulamwa" (sister in law), as she called me, "I had kept the name Sylvester for a son I would have but it seems I will never have one. Please let me give the name to my nephew". I couldn't deny Flora the joy of giving that name to her nephew so I consented wholeheartedly. True as she said, she never had a chance to get a baby because she died in January 1973, a year after getting married.

Flora's death came as a surprise. She had forced her husband to allow her to come home to the village to see us although she was sick. She stayed for a week and left for Nairobi at the end of December in 1972. She told me that she believed she was pregnant again after the two miscarriages and hoped the pregnancy would survive. Two weeks after she went back to Nairobi, word came that she was once again admitted to a hospital, bleeding heavily. She was put to sleep so the doctors could clean her uterus, but she never woke up. We have never known what happened, but there was a strong suspicion of negligence. Kenyans were not yet empowered with the knowledge of their rights. If it were now, the doctors would have been sued. Flora was the second of Daniel's sisters to die. Their firstborn Elima had died in 1968 when I was still in high school but already a 'girlfriend" or much more of a pen-pal to Daniel.

Flora's death had a great impact on Daniel. He loved his kid sister very much. He told me that she was always on his mind, and at some point, he blurted out that it was better if he died just to meet his sister Flora. I didn't take it seriously. I'd just had my second son and needed him very much. I didn't yet believe in the power of the tongue, so I left it at that. This was early 1973.

I mentioned that Flora's husband, Japheth, was a friend of Daniel's and a distant cousin of mine. Apparently, the fact that we shared some clan blood with Japheth made me an accomplice in the planning and execution of Flora's death, although I was about three hundred miles away at the time. My father-in-law called me all the bad names in the dictionary, ranging from "prostitute" to "witch," "murderer" to "good for nothing." Daniel had already gone back to

Nairobi to report for work. I tried to write letters to Daniel explaining my predicament, but he only wrote back saying that I should be patient and get to know his parents. The means of communication was bad. A mailed letter took about two weeks to get to the destination. Most communication was done by word of mouth. A messenger was sent to deliver the message. The easiest way to send letters to Nairobi was to give them to the women who went to Nairobi twice a week trading in vegetables and fruits. They would charge five Kenya shillings instead of the usual thirty cents stamps for mailing. But at least the letter arrived earlier.

When I couldn't stand the abuse by my father in law any longer, I packed my two little babies and left. My mother in law had tried to stop the insults but ended up being beaten by my father-in-law. People seemed to fear him. Many people were sympathetic but didn't really stand up in my defense. I decided to go home to my parents. They lived thirteen miles away and since there were no vehicles or any form of transportation, I walked the thirteen miles. It wasn't easy because I had Victor tied on my back, Sylvester on my chest, and a bag of our belongings on my head. It took me a long time, but I arrived safely, glad to have a mother and my adopted sister Joyce to help me with the children while I rested. I was very thin for not eating well and the stress of being blamed for things I didn't do.

I was glad I went home because after three days, one of the elders in the community—the one who had asked me to teach at Tigoi—was at it again. He wanted me to teach at Givole Primary School. I took the job and taught for one month. I went to receive my dues at Kakamega and was surprised as to how teachers, who were custodians of discipline, were fighting for their salaries. I was handed an envelope after much struggle, in which I found two hundred twenty-four Kenyan shillings, about three American dollars. There was no way I could work for that kind of money. I went home, bought my father a bed, gave the rest of the money to my parents, and only took thirty shillings for my fare to Nairobi. The fare to Nairobi by bus was only twenty-five shillings, and the commuter buses to the estates charged only fifty cents. I had four shillings and fifty cents spare, to buy food for the babies along the way.

My intentions of going to Nairobi weren't necessarily to live close to my husband. That was a secondary reason. My primary reason was to get a job and get money to support my parents as well as my husband. Apart from teaching, there were no other jobs in the village. People flocked to urban centers to get employment. I didn't see the reason why Daniel confined me to the village "to get used" to his parents. No one ever got used to his father, not even Daniel's mother. She stayed on because at that time there was hardly any divorce in Africa. Girls were socialized to obey their husbands and always submit, even when the husbands were impossible like Jacob, my father in law. Also, women who left their matrimonial homes were shunned by society. Susan, my mother in law, stayed long enough to have ten children with Jacob.

CHAPTER 10

Staying Married

A foolish woman destroys her own
house with her own hands...
—Proverbs 14:1

Growing up as a girl, I always heard the words of this scripture. In the church, in the home, and even where girls went to sleep, there was an older woman to teach them how to respect their husbands. The ultimate goal for women was marriage. A family in which girls matured before getting husbands was considered to be one of bad character—either witchcraft, theft, laziness, or selfishness. Similarly, a girl's good character was measured by how many men wanted her hand in marriage or how many people wanted her for their sons.

I grew up memorizing those teachings because I wanted to make a very good wife. My life with Daniel was routine. He got up early in the morning to take a cold shower in the public bathrooms outside the house. He found breakfast, which was mainly tea with bread and some eggs, on the table.

He went to work the whole day and came back home at nine o'clock in the night and always found his warm bath ready. Ever the good wife, I used to carry a basin full of warm water to the public bathrooms every evening. After his bath, he would eat his dinner and then go to bed. That was his daily routine, every day of the week. I got used to this routine so much that I could perform those duties with my eyes closed.

Every morning he left ten shillings on the table for the day's food. At first, I thought Daniel didn't trust me with his money. I wondered why he wouldn't even try giving me seventy shillings for the whole week. I later on figured out that he just wanted to save money, so his family wouldn't suffer in the future as he did. Because we hardly ever went anywhere together, I went to church and joined the church choir. At least every evening I would talk to other adults during choir practice.

My job-seeking efforts bore no fruits. Instead of a job, a relative of Daniel's called Peter Kibisu advised me to get further education. He was an Assistant Minister for Education, so he gave me a letter directing that I should join Kenya Polytechnic for secretarial studies. Members of parliament were very important in those days. Nobody could say no to them. I presented my school certificates and was accepted immediately. A new class was beginning in a week and I was one of the members. Peter was the pride of the whole clan of Vagisuunda. He became the yardstick of measuring how closely-related people in the clan were. You would hear "how do you refer to Peter? Is he your uncle or cousin?" From such talks, I knew that he was my uncle-in-law.

Secretarial was an interesting subject, especially when it came to shorthand penmanship. I was eager to learn the language so that I could read novels written in shorthand. There was a class called office practice that allowed us to work in offices at the Polytechnic just to have a feel of what to expect. Another one was commerce, which I didn't like very much because it involved some basic math problems.

The course was to take one year, but I was only in class for three months before I became very sick. I went to the doctor who pronounced that I was pregnant. If I was like other women who didn't suffer with pregnancies, I would have been patient enough to complete my course. But I was weak, and I didn't want to smell anything or else I would throw up immediately. I felt the same way I had when I was pregnant at Kenyatta College, hating the very air I was supposed to breathe. I quit college once again and just spent days lying in bed. Relief would come after three months when I started learning to eat like a baby. I started attending clinics in Nairobi, and I was told I was anemic. Some pills were prescribed, which were supposed to increase blood levels in the body, but they made me puke so much that I dumped them.

I was eight months pregnant when a neighbor friend of mine asked me if I needed a job. The lady was called Beatrice Musembi, or simply Mama Ndeti. She took me to the Ministry of Education and registered me as an untrained teacher. She took me to another office where I filled out an application to join a teacher training college. Hardly a week after, I received a letter to travel three hundred miles to teach in a rural school in Western Kenya, which I turned down because I was still pregnant with my third child. I also couldn't take the other two with me, or leave them with the father.

I had my baby at Pumwani Maternity Hospital, the only public maternity hospital in the whole of Nairobi. I guessed we couldn't afford the private hospitals because Daniel was saving the money. My experience at Pumwani made me swear never to go back there. Pregnant mothers were made to take a cold shower on arrival at the hospital, and all clothes, including shoes, were sent back home with the person who brought them. The mother remained in a hospital gown without shoes. They were given one pad after two hours only, so the floor was all covered in blood. Those who overbled and passed out like me had the highest chances of their babies getting swapped with stillborns or just stolen from them. The nurses were extremely abusive, and went to the point of beating women who were screaming through childbirth. They spoke English, expecting all the women who went to the hospital to be illiterate.

I remember one nurse coming to examine me and telling another nurse in English "this one is ready, but don't tell her yet." The other nurse told me to be patient because it would be another thirty minutes before I was ready. She spoke to me in Swahili. I looked at them but remained quiet as if I didn't hear them. Two minutes later, my baby was out. I thank God that I came out with my son safe and sound. I called him Felix, the name I had kept for years. This time nobody interfered with it.

Three months after delivering my baby, I received a letter from the Ministry of Education with instructions to report to Kilimambogo Teacher's College. This college is just about fifty miles from Nairobi. I knew I could come home every weekend to check on the children, but it tore my heart out to leave behind an infant under the care of a house helper and the father. All Africans love breastfeeding their babies. I cried, especially when my boobs became swollen and painful. I cried in the privacy of my bed every night, and I couldn't wait for the weekend. It was soon discovered that I didn't perform my cleaning duties at the college because I always sneaked off to see the children. I was punished, but I still sneaked away every Friday and went to Nairobi.

Daniel encouraged me all the time, and took very good care of the children while I was away. He abandoned the idea of me being a stay-home mother. He had even gone ahead and bought a sewing machine for me to learn stitching clothes for a living. He wanted to add another machine that knitted sweaters. My only problem was that I never had an interest in sewing or knitting, although I preferred knitting to sewing.

It was during one of my clandestine weekends away from college that my church choirmaster came to the house with a newspaper. It had advertisements for radio and television training vacancies.

The Kenya Institute of Mass Communication was government-owned. We didn't have to pay anything at all. In fact, the government paid us for training allowances. The church choir teacher, Solomon Mulema, had come ready with application forms. I filled out the forms and gave them to him, and on Sunday evening, I went back to college. The next time I came home, there were letters waiting for me. Daniel had already opened them but because communication those days was so bad, he had to wait for me to come home. I had been invited to attend interviews for both radio and television. The interviews took four days. I didn't go back to college but waited for the interviews. The interviews included translations of passages from English to Swahili, and some from Swahili to English, presentation of a script as they recorded it and later played it back, and then the final one would be meeting a panel of twelve very important government officers.

While other people were nervous and shaky, I just went in and did what I was supposed to do. I was a very good reader anyway, right from the school days. English and Swahili were my favorite subjects. I scored very highly in both radio and television interviews. The men and women on the panel had to ask me about my preferences. I didn't know what to choose because I didn't know what it entailed. Once again, for the second time in my life, I was confused about what to pick. The only white man on the panel, Miles Lee, was the head of radio production training. He just stood up in my presence and declared, "I want Gladys on my team," and I was glad he helped me make a decision.

College semesters in Kenya are like school semesters. Unlike in America, where students have a short break during December holidays and a break for a long summer holiday, there are three three-month terms, each divided by a one-month break. We had a break in December of 1974, and the whole family went home on a vacation. Africans never had vacations to just play and enjoy. Our vacations are for working on the farm. We drove back to Nairobi towards the end of December, only to be greeted with echoes of, "What is happening?" The names of the selected people had been announced on radio repeatedly, yet people were only used to hearing the dead being announced to inform the relatives. I didn't know whether or not to be happy. I was once again faced with a big lifetime decision to make: going back to the teacher training college or going to the mass media college and living in the same house with my husband and children. Daniel offered little help here. He told me to make the decision myself. Some people said, "This is the job you have been waiting for," while others said, "Teaching is the best profession for women." The fact that I didn't know what to expect, or what was expected of me, as a radio producer, made it worse and harder for me to make the decision. At least I knew what teaching entailed.

January 6, 1975, was the day I was expected back at Kilimambogo Teachers' College and the Kenya Institute of Mass Communication. I woke up early that morning, not knowing what to do. Daniel had already left for work, asking me to do what I thought was right. I looked at my now ten-month-old Felix and decided I would choose something that kept me close to the children. At the same time, I was already three months pregnant. I went to the Institute a bit late and asked to see Miles Lee, the Head of Radio Production Training. I told him about my doubts because I was pregnant and concerned that I might be expelled, as was the tradition in Kenya at the time.

Miles Lee was very understanding. He told me not to tell anybody else and that by the time the pregnancy showed, it would be too late for them to exclude me. The government would have invested too much in me to let go. He assured me that I had nothing to worry about, as I was legally married. I was relieved and proceeded to the class. That same afternoon, we were taken to the only Broadcasting House in the country for orientation and acclimatization.

The Kenya Institute of Mass Communication at the time was the only training center for government broadcasters in Africa South of the Sahara. It was therefore a privilege to be associated with it. Also, to be a broadcaster in Kenya at the time meant attaining celebrity status because everybody who was lucky enough to own a radio listened to the same station, since it was just one station—the government mouthpiece. There was one danger to it. The fame either formed you or destroyed you. It formed you in the sense that you could get favors, like jumping the line when paying utility bills or being let go by the traffic police when you were caught over speeding or overlapping. The worst favor was being offered free drinks, which turned many broadcasters into alcoholics, hence the branding of all broadcasters as alcoholics.

The institute was situated in the southern part of Nairobi, nearly in the suburbs. The government therefore provided a bus for transportation to and from town. There were five different classes: a radio production class, to which I belonged, television production, information and technical operators, and technicians. Each class had only six students. The radio class had four men and one more lady apart from me. We just clicked and became so close that you would think we had known each other before the institute. The other lady's name was Sally. She later became closer to me than a blood sister, but Africans have a saying that goes "when you praise a brewer too much, he or she adds water to the brew."

I was happy to have a job at long last, although I was still training for the job. We were paid a training allowance of five hundred twenty Kenya shillings per month, the equivalent of six American dollars today. The money was valuable those days. I remember us, the radio trainees, going to eat lunch worth two shillings fifty cents, only on paydays. All other days, we ate half bread and soda for a total of one shilling.

I used to call Daniel to meet me in town so I could hand the money to him, lest I get pickpocketed, and wow! Men are happy when women treat them like kings! I never knew the value of money, and my parents raised us to love God more than anything else in the world. I grew up without placing any particular importance on money. I also think it was hereditary. If I gave my father some money, he asked me why I was giving it to him. He would say, "Give it to your mother," because she was the one who made purchases. I would therefore force my father to take even ten shillings for pocket money. That is how I was.

Reflecting back on my married life to Daniel, I feel that something changed when I started bringing in a small income, and that I completely trusted him to be the man, the head of our household. I realized that he had been under stress to provide for his young and fast expanding family, and at the same time help educate his siblings, whose education had stalled due to lack of tuition fees. My training allowance was small but it made a difference.

We became closer and happier. He cut down Sundays from his overtime and made it his resting day, and then started going to church. We went to church in the morning, came back home for lunch, then went to Gikomba, the largest open-air market in Africa South of the Sahara. We bought indigenous vegetables like *mutere, zisaaga*, and *livogoi* for dinner. While I made dinner and tended to the needs of the children, Daniel took a nap the whole late afternoon. This way, he was fresher on Monday morning and throughout the week. He joined the church choir in which I sang. Life and love were on a roll!

The children were Daniel's first priority. He dearly loved his children and would do anything for them. I came second, but I didn't care because I loved the children too and wanted what was best for them. He sacrificed to buy them the most expensive clothes at the time. If I went somewhere and delayed, I had no worries, as I found the children fed, bathed, and in bed. Daniel trusted me wholly, unlike my friend Sally, who would be beaten in public by her estranged husband for shaking another man's hand in greeting. I came home with friends of the opposite sex, but my husband would just entertain them, knowing that there would never be anything else more than a mere friendship. I had many male friends. Now I know that it was psychological after having grown up as a tomboy among boys. To this day, I feel more comfortable with male friends than women because I feel that most men discuss ideas a lot of the time.

Life with Daniel was good. He was a good-natured person, never really wanting to pick on anybody. He was humble but very humorous, only to those who knew him well. At the institute, life was good too. Miles Lee, the head of radio training, and his two technicians, Ndome and Mathenge, did all they could to transform us into broadcasters. I was heavily pregnant, but everybody was supportive. Six months after the start of the training, I was getting ready to take a short leave to have my baby, and that's when hell broke loose.

I went to the office to ask for maternity leave forms, but the secretary told me to see the principal. I went to the principal's office to find out what he wanted with me. He was in a murderous state but I failed to understand what tipped him off. "You should not have started this class if you knew you were pregnant," he yelled. I just stood there staring at him. He screamed at me as I remained silent until he said he was expelling me from the course. I screamed and bolted out of his office and into Seth Adagala's office.

Seth was the head of production training for both radio and television. He loved his production team, and although the principal was his boss, they didn't get along very well. The students therefore knew how to play them. If the principal said no to something, we went to Seth, who overruled him.

I provided an avenue for them to weigh each other's strength. Seth invited me to his office and assured me that all would be fine. He left me whimpering as he headed for the principal's office. I cannot tell what happened because there was a commotion as men ran to the office. Seth was a very strong man compared to the frail principal. If they fought, he could smash the principal. Thank God, there were many men on the campus who went to stop them from fighting. Seth came back to his office where I was still sitting and scribbled a letter on a piece of paper, put it in an envelope, and gave it to me. He ordered me to take it to the Ministry of Information and Broadcasting headquarters, Jogoo House, to a man called David Olocho. I was still timid but it was a matter of life and death. I asked Miles Lee if I could be excused from the class early and he agreed that after my mission, I should go home and report to class the following morning.

David Olocho was a short stout man with a permanent smile on his face. His eyes looked very kind. Before I reached him, I had to be interviewed by his secretary, Helen, as to why I wanted to see him. She told me that Olocho was in a meeting and that I could wait or go and come back the next morning. I chose to wait. Seth had already communicated with Olocho to expect me, something the secretary didn't know. Olocho left his seat to check with the secretary and ask if she had seen me. He found me sitting at the reception, and I had been there for forty minutes. "Are you Gladys?" He asked as he ushered me in. Helen was making faces at me to warn me not to say how long I had been waiting. I just went ahead and told Olocho how the secretary had told me that he was in a meeting and that I had been waiting for forty minutes. He reprimanded Helen there and then in my presence. Helen and I would remain enemies from that point forward.

I explained my case to Olocho, who understood my dilemma. He picked up his phone and dialed the principal's number. He was the principal's boss because he was in charge of all the ministry training programs. I could hear the principal apologizing and asking that I be told to go and fill maternity leave forms. Olocho had performed a miracle. I retained my job, but I had made two enemies. Helen remained an enemy because I reported her to Olocho for keeping me waiting by lying that her boss was in a meeting when he wasn't. The principal of the Institute of Mass Communication didn't like me for reporting him to his boss at the Ministry of Information and Broadcasting headquarters. He was a very tall skinny man and a chain smoker. We used to joke that instead of crossing his legs when he sat on a chair, he wove them around each other like a rope. He never forgave me nor did he forget. But I was happy to have godfathers Adagala and Olocho. That's what everybody lived on in third world countries.

After the ordeal at Pumwani Maternity Hospital, I didn't want to see it, let alone go there to deliver a baby. We agreed with Daniel that I would go to a better hospital with the next pregnancy. I know you are wondering how many pregnancies I expected to have. My husband wanted us to raise four children but I wanted six because we were too few in my family. I was doing the fourth round, so we chose Mater Hospital. This was a hospital run by catholic fathers and sisters. Most of them were *mzungus* who were compassionate and treated patients with kindness and dignity. Another added advantage was the proximity to my college, which was only half a mile away. I would go to class, ask for permission to attend clinic checkups, and walk back to class after an hour or so. I found this to be very convenient.

CHAPTER 11

Corporation House

Unless the Lords builds the house,
its builders labor in vain.
Unless the Lord watches over a city, the
watchmen stand guard in vain.
—Psalms 127:1

Daniel worked for the East Africa Posts and Telecommunication, the savings bank branch, which was housed in Agip House, Haile Selassie Avenue, Nairobi. This was a state corporation for the three East African Countries: Kenya, Uganda, and Tanzania. The corporation had built its own living quarters and leased some in Nairobi. The company houses were cheaper and of higher quality, and it was the dream of everyone to be housed by the corporation instead of getting some minimal house allowance.

My husband Daniel had been writing endless letters to the corporation he worked for, asking to be housed. Housing has always been a problem in Nairobi, even then.

Apartments were too small and had communal bathrooms. Daniel wanted to raise his family in comfort, although he couldn't afford the more affluent apartments. East Africa Posts and Telecommunications had nice housing, but one had to know somebody who knew somebody to get one. Daniel had worked for the corporation for eight years, all the time asking for a house in vain. He was allocated one when the corporation leased some plots in the Eastleigh area on Wood Street. We rejoiced and celebrated, forgetting to thank God for the house. We moved into the house on Thursday, June 12, 1975, when I was in the last month of my fourth pregnancy. I was sure I still had about two weeks to go, but carrying items and arranging them in the new house must have taken a toll on me. Luckily enough, we didn't have much because we were moving from a small apartment, which didn't accommodate much stuff. The following day, I spent the whole day unpacking and putting stuff in place. On Saturday, I spent most of my time on the sewing machine, mending my children's clothes, although I had body aches from working too hard. We went to church as usual on Sunday and that very night, towards the wee hours of morning, I went into labor. My husband drove me to Mater hospital, and by ten o'clock, I had a baby boy.

My husband came to check on me that evening. He was happy that I delivered the baby safely, but he only stayed for three minutes. The same happened for all the four days I was in hospital. Husbands were allowed to stay till ten o'clock, and most that I saw brought goodies to their wives, but Daniel didn't bring me anything. There was no card, no flowers, no health drinks, and no food like I had seen other husbands bring. He wasn't behaving like himself. Was he unhappy that I had given him four beautiful sons? I do not know because he never said it.

My college comrades made up for what Daniel didn't do. They visited me every evening after class until I was discharged. They brought all the nice things I needed. On the fourth day, Daniel paid the bill and took me home. Just like the time I left my firstborn Victor at two weeks to go back to teach, I left my fourth-born Max at three weeks to go back to college. But it wasn't as bad as it had been when I left Felix to go to Kilimambogo Teacher Training College when he was merely three months old. At least this time I would come home every evening to see my children.

When I went back to college, everybody gave me the support I so badly needed, especially Miles Lee, who made sure that he went through what I had missed. Towards the end of July, when my baby was only six weeks old, it was time for us to go on field trips. We were given a minibus and a driver to take us to Mombasa for one full week. Before that, we wrote to companies and organizations based in Mombasa, in which we would conduct our practical fieldwork. I was scared because I didn't want to take a baby to Mombasa, and at the same time, I didn't want to leave him. As if he read my mind, Miles Lee called me to his office and advised me to do my assignments in western Kenya where I could leave the baby with my mother during the day. I was thankful. I sent letters to the Agricultural Institute in Kakamega. They wrote back, accepting my request. Going to Kakamega meant that I would have to apply for per diem, or "imprest" as we called it, because I wasn't going with the other group to Mombasa with the provided transport.

What Teaches a Flower to Bloom?

We parted ways, me moving west as the whole group went to the coast. We converged after one week to compare notes on our experiences in the field. We had all conducted very good interviews, and Miles Lee and Seth were very happy. The problem came when I surrendered the imprest. Although the principal signed the letters I sent to Kakamega before the fieldwork, he denied ever seeing them. With the animosity from the last encounter, he threatened to fire me again. This time he called me a con artist, saying that I was trying to obtain money fraudulently. I cried because I have never stolen anything in my life, leave alone trying to obtain money through false pretense.

I went to Miles Lee who tried to explain to the principal that he was the one who allowed me to do my assignments somewhere else other than Mombasa, but he wouldn't listen to him. Then I went to Seth, who intimidated him with both brain and brawn. Seth had more degrees than the principal, but things never follow the merit line in my country, or else Seth would have been the principal. I was still speaking when Seth sprang up and left the office, heading straight to the principal's office. Many people knew that the two were always fighting, so they moved closer, ready to step in and stop the fight. After yelling at the principal for frustrating his work, Seth turned to me and ordered me to go to Jogoo House again and see David Olocho. He even gave me my personal file to carry to the headquarters so Olocho could see my performance.

Because I had told Seth what had transpired with the secretary in Olocho's office, he called him to say that I was on my way. He asked me to go in directly without talking to the secretary. As soon as Helen saw me, she turned the other side and I just walked directly past her like I didn't see her. She jumped up to bar me from entering the inner office but David had seen me. He said it was ok as he ushered me to a chair. I explained my case, and the only thing he asked was whether I did any assignments. I said yes as I handed him my file.

He dialed the principal's number and asked him what he had against me. "This girl went to do official duties, which she did successfully. What else do you want from her?" he asked. The principal claimed that I tricked him into signing letters to western instead of coast. David told him that he was being held responsible for signing documents without reading them. He had failed as a senior government officer. Tables were turned. He was on the receiving end, and I couldn't have been happier. I had won another war!

I went home that evening and related the whole story to Daniel. He was thankful that there were people who reasoned differently. We were both grateful that my job had been saved again.

During the month of August, Daniel went home to the village to see the parcel of land he had purchased, and see if he could put up a small temporary house for us to sleep in when we went to the village. We never discussed his money so I didn't know that he had money to buy all the construction materials. Well, he went to Hamisi and took his father to accompany him to the land in Nandi. It was about twenty miles from the ancestral home. After Nandi on their way back to Hamisi, they stopped at Serem Market to buy all the building materials and take it to Hamisi to await the transportation to Nandi to start the construction. He later traveled to Kakamega to see his brothers, Zadock and Stephen. He didn't come back the day I expected him. He was three days late, and because the only means of communication was the mail, I had to wait patiently for him to come back.

Finally, he was dropped at our house by a public service vehicle. I noticed that he was limping while leaning heavily on a walking stick. My first thought was that he'd had an accident, but he said that this wasn't the case. He told me that his feet had started hurting him the day he bought the construction materials and took them home. He said he was in so much pain that he couldn't travel the day he was supposed to. Apart from the pain in his legs, he was losing his eyesight. According to him, he saw a cloud of darkness when he walked. We went to see an eye doctor who fitted him with eye glasses which brought him a little relief, but his legs continued to hurt. He said they felt very much swollen, although they looked normal.

The private doctors we visited didn't seem to know what was happening. When he was even just a little hungry, his whole body would shake. He was extremely thirsty most of the time, and he said he peed a lot. Yes, I know what you are thinking but there was no way we could know. Nobody thought that those were symptoms of diabetes. He struggled like that but still continued going to work every day. He lost a lot of weight, but we still didn't know what was the matter. Different doctors said he wasn't sick because they couldn't tell just by listening to his chest with a stethoscope. It made me realize that in Africa people die of preventable diseases, either due ignorance or doctors being too lazy to make the right diagnosis and put patients on the required treatment.

On the first of November, 1975, I woke up sick. I couldn't swallow anything. I know I had always been a victim of tonsillitis, but this time the pain went a notch higher. I had a very high fever. Daniel struggled with juggling his job, the children, and housework. It took me two weeks with medication to feel better. All the time we were worried about traveling to the village on the ninth of December to start our construction work on our new acquired land. Being sick was getting in the way and taking chips away from the savings intended for building purposes. Little did we know that a bigger problem was on the way! I missed college days but my professor understood that I was sick.

On the seventeenth of November, I came home from college only to find Daniel in bed, sick. I was feeling much better, but now it was his turn to be sick. I came back home from college at four o'clock as usual, and Daniel was in bed, sweating profusely. He told me he had been feeling unwell the whole day—so bad that he had to excuse himself from work. I took him to the doctor who administered malaria drugs without even running tests. We went back home, but Daniel became sicker at night. Nonetheless, he urged me to go to college because I had missed so many times with different valid reasons. Before I left, he asked me to give him a bath, which I did. I dressed him up and when I was just about to leave, he asked me to help him put his socks on. I noticed that he was sweating but his body was cold. I didn't feel comfortable to leave him alone with children, but he seemed to force me to go. I left him home with the children so as to obtain permission to be away from college.

Wednesday, the eighteenth, was my second son's third birthday. I intended to make him some chicken with ugali (corn meal), which is our delicacy. While I was cooking the chicken, Daniel said he didn't feel like eating chicken. He wished he could eat some liver. I ran to the butchery to buy liver and cooked it for him. He ate a little and vomited the whole thing. I put him to bed and went to prepare plates for the children who were hungry. We sang "Happy Birthday" for Sylvester while his dad was writhing in pain. I went to check on him, and he said he was having difficulty breathing. He wanted me to take him to hospital. Remember Solomon, the man who brought newspaper cuttings for me to apply for Voice of Kenya jobs? He came to the house at the time I was trying to look for transport to take Daniel to hospital. My intention was to take him to Mater hospital because I had been there and saw how well they treated patients. But Solomon, being a man, didn't listen to me. He ordered the driver to take us to Aga Khan Hospital.

Aga Khan was run by Asians who were not very kind to Africans. Racism was still rampant in Kenya, but we felt more at home with the whites than Asians. To this day, some Asians still treat their African domestic workers like slaves.

Daniel was admitted at Aga Khan Hospital but was never treated the whole night. On Thursday morning, I went to college to report that I had a sick person in hospital and that I would not attend class for a few days. Permission granted, I went to Daniel's workplace to report that he was sick and in hospital. By the time I went to check on Daniel in hospital it was around eleven o'clock. He was just being wheeled from the chest x-ray room back to the hospital bed. He was emaciated and breathing heavily. He said he wished he hadn't come to the hospital, as nobody looked at him. He was begging for pain medicine, but everybody ignored him. He felt like his chest was constricting, crushing his ribs and heart. He wished for death so the pain would stop. I didn't know what to do. I just sat there holding his hand as he groaned in pain.

We were waiting for chest x-ray results, hoping the doctors would attend to him. Nothing happened. He was thirsty and wanted something very cold to drink. He actually wanted a type of soda he loved to drink. I left him and went to look for the soda brand, but I didn't find it in any of the shopping areas around the hospital. I had to walk some distance, only to find two remaining bottles in a shop nearby. I bought them and walked back to hospital. Daniel grabbed the soda out of my hand like a child, asking me to open it quickly. He drank one in one gulp before he sighed. Then he drank the other one. "Thank you so much for this nice soda," he said, as if soda was something I had cooked. I sat with him until two o'clock, and then I left to go home and check on the children. After I saw the children, I walked to Jericho, a seven-mile trek, to tell my sister-in-law Rachel. We agreed to meet in town to go back to hospital and see Daniel.

At four o'clock I was standing at the bus stop in town, waiting for Rachel. We boarded a bus that took us to Aga Khan. Daniel was surrounded by two black doctors and two nurses, plus a friend of ours called Joseph who worked in the pharmacy. If anybody could save the life of Daniel, it was Joseph and a nurse called Mary—or so I thought. They worked hard, running here and there to get what the doctors wanted, pumping medicine after medicine in his drip. When they left for a while, I moved closer to feel Daniel's temperature. He was very cold. I tried to cover him, hoping he would regain body heat. Another thing was that he was becoming incoherent. He was pulling off the oxygen mask and saying things that didn't make sense.

All that time, in my naiveté, I thought he was going to be fine. I asked to spend the night at the hospital with him, but I was denied the chance. They told me to come back early in the morning. Eventually, he calmed down as if he was getting ready to sleep and we left him to rest. As soon as we were in the doorway, he yelled my name. I went back to hear what he had to say. "Take care of the children," he said and repeated it three times. He said it as he raised his head from the bed, resting on his elbow while one hand pulled down the oxygen mask. Then he sighed and lay back in bed, like he had just accomplished something. As we left the hospital ward, I thought he was going to sleep. I knew he said what he said because the children were alone in the house at that time. Little did I know that those would be his last words to me and that it would be my last time to hear his voice.

My sister-in-law and I left the hospital as she cried, lamenting that Daniel's children were too young for him to die. I didn't think that was necessary because I knew Daniel could not die. We parted ways in town, as she went to Jericho and I headed for Eastleigh. That night, I couldn't sleep at all. My second-born son kept talking in his sleep. He was telling his daddy not to go. I just remembered that Daniel had told me that he saw his late sister Flora in a dream beckoning him. I should have prayed and rebuked the evil spirit, but I didn't. If I knew then what I know now, I would have handled things differently.

I kept looking at the clock, and when it struck four, I got up, took a cold shower, and got dressed, ready to go to the hospital. Then I sat down on the couch and started crying.

I sobbed violently without knowing what I was crying for. The sobbing went on for about two hours. I felt so sad and alone. The children were still asleep, except for the fifteen-year-old house help I lived with. I know some people would think it child abuse to employ a fifteen-year-old, but it was the norm in Kenya then, and there were so many children dying of starvation. Taking one to feed, clothe, and educate was actually the best favor one could do for their family. I raised Beth like one of my children. She only left me when she attained the marriage age of twenty-one. That morning, she was awake and standing by me, not knowing what to do.

At eight o'clock, I got up, washed my face (although my eyes were swollen and red from crying), and left the house, heading for the hospital. I went down the stairs but remembered that I should let a neighbor know what was going on. We had lived in the corporation houses for four months and were still trying to warm up to each other. There was one lady, Rose, whose husband worked with mine. I was a bit closer to her than the rest. She'd had a baby two weeks prior. I went back upstairs, knocked on her door, and told her the story. She jumped into the shower and left her two-weeks-old baby to accompany me to the hospital. We boarded a bus, and sitting together, I was very quiet, but all of a sudden, Rose started talking about death. She told me that her three sons were not the only children she'd had. Her firstborn was a girl who at the age of eight months convulsed one day. Rose and her sister-in-law took her to the only private doctor in the region called Henry, walking a ten-mile distance. Henry had looked at the baby and tried to treat her but it was too late. He just told them to take the baby home. Rose's sister-in-law was carrying the baby when she died on her shoulder.

She had started crying while Rose, the mother of the baby, remained numb and silent. She just hadn't known what to do or what to say. I listened to Rose very keenly as she relived the tragic incident, teaching me a life skill.

We arrived in town and tried to cross the street and go to another bus stop where we could get another bus to the hospital. Then, I heard my name being yelled from across the street. It was Florence, wife of Joseph, the friend who worked at the hospital's pharmacy. "Daniel died last night," she yelled across the street as she crossed the street towards us. We stopped and waited for her. She just fell on me and repeatedly said, "Daniel died last night."

Florence and Rose started crying. The only thing I said was, "What will I do?" They screamed all the way to the hospital while I was quiet, listening to them. The bus conductor didn't even ask for fare. When I set my eyes on the Aga Khan Hospital, my legs suddenly became too weak to support me, and I collapsed. Some nurses came and administered first aid before I was dragged to the temporary morgue where my husband lay. He was lying there with dry tears on his cheeks. The hospital didn't even care to clean him up. It was like good riddance to them.

The picture of my husband lying there with dry tears on his cheeks has never left my mind, forty years down the line. It is still fresh in my mind as if it happened yesterday. I cry now when I think about it. I keep asking myself, "What kind of pain made him cry?" This is when I realized that God made me cry my tears beforehand because I had a hard task ahead of me. The hospital asked for their money, handing me a bill of six hundred and sixty Kenya shillings, which was like millions then. At the same time, they asked me to move the body to the City Mortuary. I didn't have any money on me. It was a Friday, and Saturdays were half working days. I had to move fast. The two women, Rose and Florence, accompanied me to the house to tell the children their daddy was no more. They hardly understood that the firstborn was only four, and we had just celebrated the third birthday for my second son two days prior to the death of his dad. Felix was one and a half years old while Max had just turned five months.

After informing the children, I walked five miles to Kimathi Estate to tell my brother, another two miles to Jericho to inform Rachel, my sister-in-law, then another four miles to Makongeni to inform my brother-in-law. I then took a bus to town and went to the offices where my husband worked. They offered to call my college and my brothers-in-law in Kakamega. It was easier because my husband worked for a telecommunication company. Otherwise, communication in Kenya at the time was terrible. My church people met with my husband's colleagues and arranged to have the body moved to the City Mortuary.

My brothers-in-law, Zack and Stephen, arrived that Friday night from Kakamega, and I breathed a sigh of relief, knowing I had helpers. I was wrong. They came with questions as to what Daniel ate last and where he ate it. There was such animosity on their part that I didn't understand how someone could insinuate that I could poison my husband to die and leave me with a problem of raising children alone. To make matters worse, I had refused an autopsy because that is what Daniel wanted. He used to say that nobody should perform an autopsy on him when he was dead. The doctor should operate on him only to save his life. When I refused an autopsy, the doctors understood because there are some religions like the Salvation Army in Africa, which do not allow autopsies on their members.

To some people, though, my refusal was an indication that I had poisoned him. From all the symptoms and the chest pain, the doctors deduced that he died of a cardiac arrest due to diabetes mellitus. In fact, he'd only needed insulin to lower his blood sugar. I am sure he would not have died if I had taken him to a different hospital, but the damage had already been done. I believe God wanted him to slip through our fingers in that way.

Saturday morning, I took my brother in law to my husband's office to get some assistance to transport the body home for burial. I gave all the money I was given to my brother-in-law Zack. The two of them left saying they were going to see if the body could be treated. Sunday, as was the tradition of the church when a member died, they converged at my home for a service and fundraising to assist us. At two o'clock when the service was going on, my brothers-in-law came in with the body, ready to transport it without my knowledge and consent. I was young and naïve. I had even given them the burial permit, and they used it and the money I gave them to fight me.

It is the norm for the body to be taken to the house that the deceased used to live in before transportation upcountry. I don't know why, but it is a culture that has been too hard to abandon. The church had to cut the service short as we gathered the children on the bus. My brothers-in-law gathered everything from my house, starting with the beds, all the furniture, all the cooking utensils, the stove, the radio, the beddings, the little food there was, and anything they could lay their hands on. In short, the house was eventually as clean as we found it when we first moved in.

The bus traveled overnight, arriving at Hamisi on Monday morning. Relatives hadn't even been informed of Daniel's death when his brothers decided that he had to be buried on Tuesday. The whole saga surrounding Daniel's death, the way he was neglected in hospital, him having dry tears on his cheeks, and the brothers wanting him buried immediately, has remained one of the saddest, most haunting memories to me. Daniel was a good man, so why did people treat him like a criminal, even in death? It would have been understandable if he was a Muslim because their religion demands the dead to be buried immediately. In fact, I wish all religions had that same rule, but Christians are different. The body has to be kept for a number of days as all the relatives are called to come and witness the burial. Before the coming of morgues, the bodies were kept under the eaves of their house for at least three days. I would have liked to keep Daniel for days on end because I had not yet registered his death in my mind. It was very, very painful.

Daniel's body wasn't taken to the church for a requiem mass as it would be these days. The service was staged at home, with pastors sitting under a shelter made from papyrus reeds, while the rest sat on the ground in the hot sun. Some women carried umbrellas, but they were useless, as people sitting behind them shouted at them to fold their umbrellas, as they were obscuring the speakers, especially when I stood to give a history of his illness, which was very short. You could hear sobs and sniffs in the crowd when people saw how young I was with very young children. I told them that Daniel had not been sick for long. It was a shock to me, and that I would not make it alone without the presence of Jesus Christ wherever I went. I asked for prayers and sat down.

It was when I sat down that a sight struck me. I saw my college mates in the crowd. Sally was there, but it was Morriex Muteti whom I saw first because he was very brown. We used to call him "yellow bastard," a term that we read from a South African textbook called *Mine Boy*. He called me a Dinka from South Sudan because of my dark complexion. Ben Muriithi, now Issa, Geoffrey, Polycarp, and others from other classes like television production and technical. Apparently, the college had virtually closed due to Daniel's death.

Seth authorized transport to get students to the funeral. Their sight comforted me. I was so relieved to see them. It seemed like they had brought a solution to my problems. I realized that having friends to visit during a time of need is very important. That visit cemented my closeness with my fellow students at the Kenya Institute of Mass Communication, including those who had graduated earlier. Reality set in after the burial and after my colleagues left for Nairobi. I sat alone with my babies like a leper. People still believed in myths that sitting close to a newly widowed woman could make your wife or husband die.

My sisters-in-law by marriage were also worried that I would snatch their husbands, now that I had become single. My mother-in-law, who had been close to me, started believing the rumors that I could have caused her son's death and stayed aloof. In fact, I started doubting my sanity. Was I really to blame for my beloved husband's death? I may have imagined it, but everybody looked angry at me. Even the sky, which was normally blue with scattered white clouds, was grey, with the sullen clouds looking pregnant with moisture. It was going to rain. It would rain on the mound of red earth covering Daniel, the man I loved, the father of my now crying children, nestling against me as if fearful that something would take me away from them.

I thought about the last moments with him. Just five days ago, he was alive and well, and now he is nowhere to be seen. The most affected of the children was Victor, who was four. At least he knew his dad. He still remembers him, however vaguely. Sylvester was exactly three years old and was very close to his father because of having been sickly. The other two boys, Felix and Maxwell, were too young to notice anything. It killed me when Sylvester went through the crowd looking for his father. He clung to my brother-in-law Zack who resembled Daniel, but he was in no mood of comforting a bereaved child. He would shove him away and pick up his own daughter. His wife was very watchful, lest I steal her husband.

Thank God for my sister Truphena, who braved the tradition to stick with me. But there came a time when she had to go to her home, as she lived upcountry while her husband lived in Nairobi. Her husband wasn't enthused about sticking close to me. As I write this book, forty years after, my brother-in-law Manase is still a strong church elder while the women who ran away from me are long-widowed now. I don't want to claim it divine retribution. I am simply stating a fact of how sometimes traditions are misplaced.

My mind wandered to the one-roomed apartment in Pangani. It had been so peaceful. Did we really have to move to a corporation's house? Perhaps Daniel would not have died. Why did he die just five months within our moving?

Those were the questions I asked myself, but of course I got no answers. I was thinking aloud, but the hurt in my heart was too deep to bear. Crying didn' help as people say. To this day as I write this story, I can feel my emotions welling up like the whole thing just happened. However, the real saga hadn't even begun.

CHAPTER 12

The Struggle

*Naked I came from my mother's womb
and naked I will leave this life.
The Lord gives and the Lord takes away.
Praise the Name of Yahweh . . .*
—Job 1:21

It hurt so much to think that Daniel grew up in abject poverty, struggled all his life, hoping to live happily someday, but it never happened. He shivered every time he imagined that his children could live the same life as he lived. All his struggles had been geared towards making a better life for his children than he had had. He had bought them every luxurious thing he thought he missed in life. I shed tears of pity when he related to me the first time he earned a salary, which went towards his brother Zack's tuition. Zack had been out of school a whole year for lack of fees. The only thing Daniel got out of his first salary was his fare to and from work for a month, which was hardly equivalent to five dollars (five hundred Kenya Shillings). He also took his brother to Burma market in Nairobi to eat lunch of ugali and chicken, and buttered bread and soda afterwards. Those were the things he had craved while living with his brother Javan and his family in Mbotela, Nairobi.

Living with their brother Javan was hell. He, his wife, and three children would eat bread without offering any to his younger brothers. His life was more or less the same as mine under Lily's roof. At one time, he had to run away to live with his friend Kisangi, who lived with his father while his mother was in the village. Daniel persevered and made it through school, although he didn't complete tuition payment. He wouldn't be issued a certificate until he paid for it in full by himself. His first priority was to take his brother back to school. Only after doing so, he bought clothes for himself and made a point of eating well.

Growing up, radios and record players were very scarce. Only the affluent could afford those things. As much as the youth loved music, Daniel's brother wouldn't allow him to touch his radio. One of his first assets was a radio, and he later crowned it with an automatic radiogram, which could change vinyl records automatically. Most of his friends envied him for his achievement.

Daniel had this idea of women not working outside the home. It was his desire for me to be a stay-home mother to raise children. While doing that, he imagined I would be bored so he bought a Singer Sewing machine for me. Unfortunately, I wasn't so domesticated. Needlework was never part of my plan. I loved cooking because I learned it from my mother, but anything else that women were assigned by gender rules was out of my vocabulary. The other thing he bought before he died was a typewriter, for me to practice my typing skills when I had a stint at secretarial training at the Kenya Polytechnic. I didn't complete the course because I became pregnant with Felix and forgot the whole thing. Daniel loved sleeping comfortably. He bought nice beds for everyone in the house, including his children and the house help. The mattresses and beddings were nice too.

The kitchen was well equipped with good chinaware as well. His wardrobe was up to date, and his children—our children—were well dressed. Food was no longer our problem. By the time he died, we were happy, with his good salary and my training allowance which supplemented the income. We loved and we laughed.

Perhaps the biggest investment was the ten-acre land he bought in Nandi County on which to settle his family. He had gone home to prepare building material for a home on the farm when he came back to Nairobi, limping on a cane. We had planned to start the building process in December of 1975, but he passed on in November.

Daniel died, leaving all his possessions on earth behind and is relatives viciously fought over them. I cannot tell you who took the sewing machine, who grabbed the radio, or who took the typewriter. His clothes were even fought over. A few people had dispersed to their homes while others stayed behind because it had started raining heavily. Normally, the Luhya tribe believe that when it rains after one's burial, it means he or she has been accepted into heaven. While Daniel had been accepted to enter heaven, there was a struggle in the home over the sweat of his brow. Some were bleeding after being hit hard on the head for clinging to something somebody else wanted.

The following day, after spending the night with my children alone in the house, I woke up to see the grave, and my heart ached for Daniel. I had not even made breakfast for my children when my father-in-law came to the house blaming me for hiding some of my husband's possessions. He didn't believe that what they shared the previous day were all that Daniel had left. After screaming at me at the top of his voice, he went away and brought two men with him, who helped him take out the building material Daniel had bought. It had all been stored in one of the rooms in our three-bedroom house in the village. I let them do it. When the material, which included corrugated iron sheets for roofing, some wooden doors and window frames, and all the nails had been taken out, he went to look for a buyer. At this juncture, one of my brothers-in-law, Caleb, who was bleeding the previous day for having been hit hard, came to me, offering his alliance. He had been offered the not-so-good remainder of the loot, so he wanted to hit back. He told me to wake up and stop crying. He said that his father was going to sell those things if I wasn't careful. To tell the truth, I didn't even care, but now that he mentioned it, I decided to fight back. I asked him what I could do. He went back to the shopping center and came with a truck. The owner wanted only two hundred shillings, the equivalent of two dollars but which was still a lot of money then. Caleb asked me if I could afford it, and I said I could because people had been squeezing money into my hands for consolation. He said we had to load the building material and take it to Nandi before his father, my father-in-law, came back with a buyer. There were neighbors in Nandi, who were our neighbors in Hamisi before they moved, and they agreed to safekeep the material.

They knew what my father-in-law was capable of. We put all the material in the house of the woman called Elizabeth. The truck was going back to Hamisi, so we rode back together.

Everything was quiet when we arrived at home at around six o'clock in the evening. I went to my house, where my children were huddled together with my house help. It had started raining heavily again.

It was still raining at around seven o'clock when a sudden bang on the door occurred, followed by a yell asking, "What are you doing in my house, prostitute?' My father in law was calling me a prostitute and other profanities. The children started screaming. The door was kicked open as my father in law came in rushing towards me in the kitchen. "Where is the money?" They asked as they punched and boxed me. My father-in-law noticed I was wearing Daniel's watch on my wrist. He grabbed my arm and twisted it as he tore off the watch. I was holding my baby Maxwell on my lap but they didn't seem to care. Jacob, my father-in-law, grabbed him and threw him outside through the window. As I rushed to take the baby, I was screaming for help. Many people came to witness the scene but never helped. I was fighting with four men. Caleb, my only ally, had been hit on his knee and paralyzed. My sisters-in-law by marriage, wives to my brothers-in-law, were in their houses, watching through the windows, some laughing. When I thought I could be killed and leave my children, I urged my house help to take the children outside as I carried the younger two. We left the home in the rain and darkness. Nobody sympathized with us except one old woman who took us into her round mud hut. We didn't care that it was smoky. I left the children there and walked about eight miles to seek help from my uncle-in-law, who seemed reasonable.

After I walked all that way, the man, whose name was Absalom, said it was too late and raining, and that I should just go back home. He would come to solve the matter in the morning. I realized people feared Jacob. Why wouldn't they fear him? He had once hit his brother Peter on the head with a hammer, nearly killing him. For that, Jacob was imprisoned for only six months, and he often bragged about it. I guess that's why nobody was willing to interfere with the fights in his home. Disappointed, tired, wet, and hungry, I walked back all the way, groping in darkness and crying. I came back after midnight, soaked from the rain.

That night, the woman who took us in put some of her old clothes on the floor and put my babies to sleep. When I came back, she warmed some water, added salt, and massaged me with an old piece of rag. It eased my bruises a bit. Early in the morning, even with my fractured wrist, I took my children and walked the thirteen miles to my mother's home. I didn't walk because I wanted to. It was because there was no public transport from Hamisi to Tigoi. One walked the nine miles to Majengo and took a *matatu* the remaining three miles. There were other shortcut paths that could take you direct to Tigoi without having to walk to Majengo first, but I preferred the road for safety and also hoping against hope that a ride would appear from nowhere.

One other thing I would like to say is that the old lady who took me in the previous night lived a lonely life. People shunned her because her husband had died and all six of her children too. She had no family. The villagers labeled her a witch and feared her. It was therefore surprising that the "witch" was the only person merciful enough to help me, when nobody else would, for fear of being reprimanded by Jacob, or whatever reasons they had. She became my other mother from that time until her demise six years later.

My parents, especially my mother, was so distraught to see me in such bad shape. The children were hungry and tired. My mother knew the power of water. She prepared a hot bath for me as well as the children, while she cooked. The children ate and went to bed early, leaving me to relate the ordeal. My cousins wanted to form an army and go to Hamisi to wreak havoc, but my mother, being prayerful, urged them to leave it to God.

It was very hard on me to have lost my husband at the age of twenty-five with four children to raise, only to get beat up by his family and have everything taken from me, including some of my clothes and the children's. I didn't have any money at all. My purse had been snatched from me during the struggle because they knew that was where the money was. The other problem with those people was that they wanted to bar me from inheriting any money from my husband. They all had a claim to his estate but audaciously said that the children were not theirs. They claimed that I was a prostitute and had other men sire the children, whom I then claimed were Daniel's. The children therefore had no right to get anything from their father's death. So, here I was, bereaved and thrown out of the home.

I was at my parents' home for one week when my mother-in-law came. She claimed to have come to see how the children and I were doing, but the real reason was to plead with me to go back home so they could make peace. I must have been wrong. They had other ideas. Apparently, people had made them a laughing stalk for beating up a widow and throwing away their own son's children. My mother-in-law pleaded with me to go back to finish the mourning period before I was allowed to leave the home. I refused. But when she mentioned that it would affect the lives of my children, as it was customary, I had to reconsider. I had lost my husband and I wasn't ready to lose any of my children. I gathered them and went back to Hamisi with my mother-in-law. My brother-in-law, Caleb, the only one on my side, had informed the district administration about the case. They had consequently sent two police officers to stand guard.

They put a restraining order on any of the men in the family from entering my house, except Caleb. Although I was safe from the beatings, I had to endure the insults and ridicule. I persevered in order to do what tradition demanded. For two weeks, I listened to abuses and insults. When I was done and was getting ready to go back to Nairobi, I woke up one morning to find people in the home working frantically as if there was supposed to be a ceremony in the family. I didn't understand what was going on because very few people talked to me, and I found solace in remaining in my house most of the time.

Relatives who lived far away had arrived. Chairs were being arranged in the front yard, and food was being cooked by women from the village. I didn't ask what it was all about because I knew the question would be answered by insults. At noon, I saw some well-dressed people, according to the village standards, come into the compound. Some women carried paper bags in which to carry food back home. I recognized some people as church members where my parents-in-law worshipped. I watched through my window as people took their strategic seats. I observed silently. All my brothers in law and even their cousins were present. Then I was invited to the meeting. After prayers and adoration, a pastor preached, saying what they were about to do was written in the bible, and that Ruth, who clung to Naomi, had passed through the same process. I didn't care and I didn't understand. I had checked God out for taking my husband from me, and I was very angry with Him.

Then one clansman stood, gave a speech, and asked all the brothers in law to stand. I was told to stand up and pick one of them to take over Daniel's husbandly duties. I was shocked. I remained quiet. They called me a hundred times, but their calls fell on deaf ears. The clansman stood again and asked all the cousins to stand and join my brothers-in-law. He said, "If you think your brothers-in-law are not good enough for you, choose from the cousins," adding that it was a tradition for a widow to be inherited. I stood up, all eyes on me, and opened my mouth to utter four words, which were "Love cannot be transferred," as I walked away to my house. If the policemen had not been present, I would have been killed that day.

I heard choruses of curses behind me, some saying I had been rude to the clan elders, and that it was a grievous mistake that would make me die. My sisters-in-law, sisters to my husband, joined in. They yelled profanities. They concluded that I had actually been the cause of my husband's death, the real reason why I didn't want to be "inherited."

The tradition of a brother taking over his sister-in-law was formed long time ago. Women in Africa depended mostly on husbands, as the culture is purely patriarchal. When a man died, the clan had to provide somebody respectful to help raise the orphaned children. Some men just provided for the brother's children without having to engage in living together as husband and wife. I had my education, and I knew that once I completed my course, I would be able to feed my boys. Moreover, I was still devastated by my husband's death, and no man mattered to me anymore. I sat silently in my bedroom, listening to their ranting of how rude I was and their curses. The children were playing outside with their cousins, oblivious to what was going on. The people in the home were more civil to the children than they had been a week ago. They hoped to win my favor through the children. I started piecing things together and finally concluded that even Caleb was nice to me because he thought he would easily inherit me. I noticed that he was one of the more than ten contestants. Caleb, though a qualified plumber, was always jobless because he always drunk too much with the first salary and forgot to go back to work. He had been fired several times. Javan, too, was retired due to alcoholism. They all lined up to get me in the hope that they would be employed in Daniel's place, if they said they were taking care of his family.

One voice of a woman suggested that I be dragged out of the house. Another one quipped, "Can't you see the security here?" At that moment, I just made up my mind to leave and never to come back. I gathered the few clothes that had been spared for me and my children. I called the children in and told them to be ready to go. They were unhappy, as they had started warming up to their cousins, but we had to go. I called a neighbor's son who was passing by through the window and asked him to carry my small bag of belongings.

He agreed, and so I grabbed the children as if I was taking them to the house, but I was actually leaving unseen, via the back door. At the shopping center, some people sympathized and told me to go away. Some went to call my mother-in-law. I was still wondering how to carry my babies when a vehicle came.

Surely God knows those who are in trouble. The car was heading to Kisumu and the owners, a kindly man and woman, gave me a ride to Tigoi. They knew who I was and had been to the funeral. They didn't even ask for fare. They were so touched by my state that the woman was crying as she recalled how cruel my family-in-law had been. I have never met that couple again. Sometimes I feel like they were angels sent from above to rescue me.

I went back to my mother's home. I didn't know that my sneaking away could become my mother-in-law's problem. She was reprimanded by the clan people and beaten by my father-in-law, accusing her of allowing me to escape. From that time, my mother-in-law, Susan, became my ally. She was also thrown out of the home. I failed to understand what sons would allow something like that to happen to their mother, just because they wanted to inherit their late brother's wife. Susan also spent a night at a neighbor's house and left early in the morning for Tigoi. I couldn't believe what an animal my father-in-law was when I saw the bruises she had on her body. My mother applied the traditional African first aid, giving her a warm bath and some food. After three days, she was much better. I decided to take her with me wherever I went. We became like the biblical Ruth and Naomi. I took her with me back to Nairobi.

My parents gave me money for the trip. I was accompanied by my mother and mother-in-law. I had to go back to college. The two mothers came with me, one for having been thrown out of the home, and the other, my mother, didn't think I was able to take care of the children on my own, after what I had been through. My father was jobless at the time but had a lot of livestock. He sold one of his cows and gave me all the money to travel back to Nairobi and try life with the children on my own.

I prepared to go to Nairobi by washing the few belongings I had after everything was taken from me. It skipped my mind that I was going back to a house that was left empty after the looting by my family-in-law. There was one sister-in-law, Tabitha, who would kill for earthly belongings. She fought for everything that would benefit her. She was on the front line with the brothers in insulting and beating me up.

Rachel also blatantly told me that the men I slept with had poisoned her brother. She said her brother only ate at home, and since he died of food poisoning, I must have been the one who planned his death. Jessica was the only sister-in-law who didn't utter an insult against me. Her problems were bigger than mine. She'd had five children with four different fathers who had abandoned her, and she lived in the home with her children. She was careful not to say anything that might jeopardize her life in the home. To understand a little more about my husband's family and why his mother found it safer to run away and accompany me to Nairobi, perhaps I should tell you a bit more about my father-in-law.

According to my mother-in-law, Susan, her husband Jacob, was a greedy man who always acted on impulse but never regretted his actions, even when they hurt those around him.

Jacob had two brothers: Peter, the oldest, and Nathan, who was the middle child. Peter was a police officer with the then East African Community, based in Dar Es Salaam, Tanzania. Living far away only allowed him to come home once a year, for a month during his leave days (vacation). During this time, Peter would bring home all the wealth he had acquired during the year and leave it home in the care of his brothers as he went back to his job. Jacob would greedily pounce on those things, which included clothes, building materials, tools, and anything else he might acquire. Living up to the meaning of his nickname, 'Grabber', Jacob eventually took Peter's land too, and as if that wasn't enough, he even took Peter's younger wife and had a baby boy with her by the name Stephen. To sleep with a brother's wife is taboo in the Maragoli cultural mores. The elders sat and decided to send the wife packing, but Jacob took the boy and gave him to Susan to raise with her other children. He became very close with Zack and lived in Kakamega.

When Peter retired from the police force, he found that he had no land to settle on. Instead of fighting Jacob, he left the land to him and bought another piece on which he built a home. One day when he came visiting, Jacob mistook his visit to mean that Peter wanted to ask him about his wealth he had squandered. He rushed out of the house with a hammer and clobbered his brother Peter on the head amid screams from family and neighbors. Jacob was still struggling to finish off his brother, even after he lay on the ground unconscious. Luckily for Peter, our home is right next to the Hamisi dispensary, where first aid was ministered to him before he was rushed to Kisumu Hospital. Jacob was jailed for six months, something that embittered him greatly. Peter eventually forgave him and wanted a relationship with his brother, but Jacob never accepted him back in his life. He still expected Peter to come kneeling to him, as if he was the one that was aggrieved. They both died without talking to each other, Nathan having died earlier in a road accident.

I was putting all that behind me and walking into the future. I didn't know what held tomorrow but I sure knew who held tomorrow in His Hands.

CHAPTER 13

Back to Nairobi

For you will not leave in a hurry, and you will not run; because the Lord is going before you, and the God of Israel will be your rear guard ...
—Isaiah 52:12

I had left Hamisi in a hurry twice, one time beaten and chased from the home with my children being thrown out of the house into the rain. This time, I did what I could to distance myself from these detractors. But I had been convinced by my mother-in-law to adhere to the norms, beliefs, and values, to go back and finish the mourning period for my beloved husband. I felt that he had been aggrieved and died too early, and that anything I did in his honor would make him happy wherever he was. I had gone back to Hamisi of my free will. The second time, I had to run and leave in a hurry, because the cultural demands that were being made on me were too much for me to bear. To be forced into a marriage with a man I didn't love just wasn't something I could live with.

Here I was, now leaving in style for Nairobi, with no money but armed with freedom from the mean people. My father and my cousins saw us to the bus stop. A *matatu* took us to Kisumu where I decided that we would take a small vehicle, a seven-seater, which was faster. We needed to arrive early in the day so we could think about sleeping arrangements. I had earlier sent a telegram to my church pastor, informing him of my intentions to come back to Nairobi. He had assembled church members and asked them to donate whatever they could. They also cleaned the house. When we arrived, the church members were there. We had a short service in honor of Daniel and prayers for the widow and the orphans. All asked God to take care of the orphans as he promised in his good book. The house, which had been completely empty, now had a few blankets, bedsheets, plates, and cups, as well as foodstuff. There were no mattresses, but that was alright. The church members had cooked some food—enough to last us till the next day. For the next month, I was fed by friends and neighbors, some who had heard of Daniel's death too late to attend the funeral. Anybody that came to console us brought either food or money, and sometimes both. I felt comforted but the loss of Daniel, my life companion, was too overwhelming for me.

Every Saturday, I sat next to a window to watch people come from work at the time Daniel came home, and started crying. I had the urge to cry all the time. Some people told me that it was good to cry while others told me to stop crying because the children would sense the trouble and pine away. Whatever they said, it took a lot of time. Whatever they said, Daniel's death remained fresh in my mind. It is 45 years today as I write this book, but tears are rolling down my cheeks.

I was getting comfortable in the house and beginning to get the feel of life after Daniel, when one day there was a knock on the door. It was exactly three months since the death of Daniel, and two months since I came back from his burial, because I was away in the country for one month. At the door were two men from the post office corporation with a seven-day notice to vacate the corporation house. I pleaded with them that I didn't have anywhere to go—to no avail.

My mother had only stayed with us for two weeks only and since returned to the village. My mother-in-law stayed on for lack of where to go, and I allowed her. But my sister-in-law Rachel, who didn't understand our connection, wasn't thrilled about her mother living with me. She moved her to her house when it became serious that I had to vacate the house. She offered no help. I was once again on my own. Seven days later, I was being thrown out of a home. The people from the corporation came and threw out the belongings. Thank God I didn't have beds and mattresses and other furniture. The men were so ruthless. I tried to protest, but one of them retorted, "You don't work for us, so you can't occupy our house," and added, "If life is too hard for you in the city, you might consider going back to the village." At the mention of the village, tears welled in my eyes, and I sobbed uncontrollably. The seven men didn't see my tears, nor did they feel my pain. They locked the door after making sure everything was out of the house. I had nowhere to go but make a sleeping place on an open space near the staircase. I lived there for three weeks. I cooked there in a corner on a kerosene stove, washed clothes at a community water faucet, and begged for places to take a shower.

I used to leave in the morning to go to college, looking haggard and come back in the evening. Very few people knew what was going on until I confided in my college mates. Their brains went to work immediately to see how they could help me. I remember one lady offering me a place to live as long as I didn't bring the children along. I felt insulted. I wasn't going to stoop so low as to abandoning my children for a place to lie. At this juncture, Sally offered to be a roommate, if we could get a house to share. My brother Jairus came by every day to see me. He could have been of help, but they lived in a small apartment—about six of them. He went around asking for a vacant room. His workmates had houses all over Nairobi, and one of them in Uhuru Estate Phase 3 was falling vacant. My brother informed me about it, and I talked to Sally. She agreed, and we moved in together in March of 1976.

The house had two bedrooms. Sally and her daughter took one, and I got the other with my children. The kitchen was large enough for our house help to sleep in. We shared the kitchen, living room, toilet, and bathroom. The rent for this house was six hundred Kenya shillings, the equivalent of six dollars a month. It didn't look like much, until you considered the training allowance of five dollars that each of us received on a monthly basis. Fifty cents went to water and electricity bills. Our balance was a dollar fifty cents for the two families to live on for the whole month. I cannot even explain how we made it through the month.

While this was going on, I had another war to fight at the college. My friend the principal was at it again. Because I had been away for a month after my husband's death, he believed I had not grasped anything at college. The only solution was to be discontinued. He was so serious that I didn't even recognize him. He asked me to leave the compound and never come back. That was the first day I went to college after returning to Nairobi. Instead of leaving the compound, I went to Seth Adagala's office crying. Seth had been the one who authorized transport to ferry students to the funeral. He knew what was going on. To hear that I had been expelled from college infuriated him. He ordered me to stop crying and take action. He said, "I showed you David, the head of training in the ministry. Go to him and report everything." He gave me a file and sent me to Jogoo House to see David Olocho once again. This was going to be the third time.

At the office, the secretary who didn't like me was out for lunch. There was a different one standing in for her. She let me in immediately. One thing I had come to like about Olocho was that he was a good listener. I related the whole story to him, and he put everything aside to listen. Still, I didn't know that he was from the same tribe as me. I believed he was a Luo, and he thought I was a Luo too. The Luos, who are mostly fishermen, come from the region around Lake Victoria. We are Luhyas from western region of Kenya. Both of us, along with Seth, came from the same sub-tribe of Maragoli. Although this was the case, Olocho used to help anybody without caring where he or she came from.

After I'd told my story, Olocho took his phone and dialed the Kenya Institute of Mass Communication. Talking to the principal, he said, "Mr. Principal, I have a lady in my office, and this is the third time she has been here. She says you have expelled her from college. Is that so?" I heard the voice from the other end say that it was so, and it was because that woman had not attended college. She has been playing around, missing classes. Olocho asked, "Did you know her husband died?" He said he knew, but the time I took off was too long. Olocho said it would have been better to talk with Seth and Miles Lee, the instructors, to find out if she could continue or not. Then he gave a ruling: "She will remain in class until I have written and signed statements from those two instructors, and I will go by their word."

I went back to college, and at the close of day, the messenger had delivered the statements. I got to have copies, and they were all praises on how I had been resilient despite the problems I had faced. I was therefore allowed to continue from where I'd left off, as Miles Lee had a soft spot for me. The technical operators were not so good. Ndome was good, but Mathenge treated me unkindly. I later came to discover that he was carrying out orders from the principal to frustrate me out of the course. I had my children to think about, and so I worked double hard.

We graduated from the Kenya Institute of Mass Communication in March of 1975. We joined the workforce at the Voice of Kenya, all the while still receiving the training allowance of five hundred shillings, an equivalent of five dollars per month. My children were starving. We ate one meal a day. My youngest baby, almost a year old now, was crying all the time. I knew it was hunger, but I had nothing to offer. My brother, who had always supported me, had mortgaged his salary and could no longer sustain himself.

Sally decided to do what other women do: find a man who could provide. I had no time for entertaining men. I divided the only time I had between my children and my job. I had long abandoned God, who I thought had let me have all the problems in the world. I didn't see sense in worshipping

God, who was partisan, giving some people all the blessings while pouring curses on others. I kept asking what I had done to deserve all that was happening to me. Little did I know that God is never asked questions. His decisions are final.

When I thought that I could bear it no longer, I wrote a letter to the Director of Broadcasting, Mr. James Kangwana, asking him to transfer me to Kisumu, a city near my home village so that my mother could help me feed my babies. Plus, I thought that life in the village would be much cheaper. On receipt of my letter, Kangwana called me to his office and told me that the commendation I received from the Institute was too strong to let me go to the village. At the same time, he said that promotions come to the head office and those in outside stations can easily be forgotten.

Kangwana was a godly man. He talked to me about people who passed through what I was experiencing only to become very important in society. He assured me to hang on and that all would be well. As I left his office, I was both happy and disappointed. My children were still hungry. I remember only having enough money to buy a packet of milk. I would divide the milk into four equal parts and give them to the babies for dinner. I would ask them to drink a lot of water, which would make their bellies full. Life was hell on earth. I very much treasured the moments I would meet somebody I knew on the bus, who would pay my fare of fifty cents. I knew I had spared the money to buy milk.

I decided to see Miles Lee and tell him that I had problems and I was on the verge of a mental breakdown. I walked through life like a zombie, never talking unless necessary and never smiling. I used to be humorous but not anymore. Jokes were for those who could afford food for their children. Miles referred me to Seth, and as usual, Seth sent me to Olocho. This time, Olocho listened to the problem and sent me to another man who was in charge of housing in the Ministry of Information and Broadcasting. The man recommended that I be paid a provisional house allowance of three hundred shilling, pending our appointment. We had been in limbo for three months, having completed our training, but not yet appointed to the job posts. That eased my problem but not enough to feed four young children and the house help.

It wasn't until October of 1976 that we were appointed to our designation and our salaries were reviewed. At least we got to the point of earning one thousand eight hundred shillings, plus three hundred house allowances. That made it two thousand one hundred shillings, which was about two hundred and ten dollars. Under our first president, Jomo Kenyatta, there was no inflation. Food prices were at their lowest, and with that salary, I made sure I fed my children and even spared a little money to support my parents and pay the house help.

I was beginning to enjoy myself when I nearly made the biggest mistake of my life. I have lived to regret every moment but glad that I was unable to accomplish it. The story is long but all the same important because it changed the trajectory of my life with my sons.

Daniel didn't live long enough to take his children to school, something he looked forward to with his entire mind. He died when Victor, the firstborn, was just four years old. Daniel's sister Rachel was a nursery school teacher. Since I couldn't afford the pre-school tuition, I tried to ask my sister-in-law to make it possible for Victor to join St Joseph's

Nursery School, Jericho, because a teacher could have his or her child attend the facility free. Rachel didn't have small children anymore. She refused to help me, adding, "You should have known better before you killed my brother." I was offended to the core. I didn't kill my husband, and my children were theirs too. I cried and walked away.

The following day I went to see the Father in charge of the church and school. After I related the story, he was very touched. Father Thomas was a very kind man, who spoke with a slight foreign accent. I never asked where he came from. He sympathized with me but said he couldn't educate the child for free. I would have to pay half the fee, which was the equivalent of today's two dollars instead of five dollars per month. If you remember, I was still earning the equivalent of five dollars a month.

While I was still mesmerized with the kindness of the Catholic Father, he added "And if you have other children, I will treat them the same." That meant that all my children would pass through St Joseph's at half price. I was so grateful to the Father. Rachel was shocked to see my son in the class she taught. Because she wanted to show the world that she was close to the late brother's children, she started acting good to them. She would take Victor to her house, and then I would pick him from there after work. I was always accompanied by Sally. The arrangement worked well for a while. However, one evening, Sally and I got to Rachel's house and heard loud voices from inside. I shuddered as the chill of premonition passed through my body, but I didn't know why.

We knocked at the door, but those inside were too engrossed in their conversation to hear the knock. I pushed the door open and there they were: my father-in-law and two of my brothers-in-law! Apparently, as I learned later, Rachel had invited them to come and accost me for killing Daniel, and take all the money he'd left behind. It is mandatory for Africans to shake hands when they meet, but my father refused my handshake when I extended it to him. His sons did the same. Victor came from the kitchen and held onto my skirt.

Then Rachel started the insults. "Gladys has become a prostitute and even sleeps with Mzungus. How did Father Thomas give her free education for her child if that is not the case?" she said. Then, the insults came pouring from all their four mouths, without giving me a chance to explain anything or defend myself. Sally ran away, leaving me behind with my son. I'm sure she didn't want to be caught up in a dysfunctional family's dispute. I just stood there crying as I held to my son's hand as if for protection.

My father-in-law stood up and hit me on the cheek, but that was after he said it all, as Rachel fanned the fire. The sons stood up as if in a choreographed sequence and each held my arms as they threw me out of the house. I landed in a heap of charcoal. Neighbors had heard the shouting and came to gather around the house, but my attackers weren't done. They came and punched me and would have continued had somebody not come to my rescue. The curious crowd just watched the exciting scenario with deep interest, most of them following me as the man who'd come to my aid walked me down the street away from Rachel's house. He only left me when he was sure I was safe. I walked with my son to the house, which we shared with Sally, crying all the while.

I pulled myself together and made supper for the children, but I couldn't eat a single mouthful. We used to sing, dance, and pray after dinner but this time there was nothing of that sort. Earlier when I went to the butchery to buy some meat, I had also gone to the store to buy insecticide. My eyes were red from crying. The shopkeeper handed me the insecticide as he joked that the mosquitoes and mice I was going to kill must have kept me awake the previous night. I just smiled without saying anything. We used to joke around, but he was surprised that I just smiled and walked away. He called after me to take the change I was forgetting. As I went back for it, he tried to ask if anything was the matter, but I assured him that all was fine. I went home and waited for the children and our house help to sleep before I did what I wanted to do.

When it became convenient, I took a large jug, poured out the entire bottle of insecticide, and broke two size D batteries in the contents. This caused a reaction and fizzed, but I was happy that it would work just fine. Somehow, everyone went to bed quite early and I was left alone to do the grim thing I intended to do. I was crying all the time. I was fed up with everything. I just wanted to drink the concoction with my children and die so we wouldn't face anymore beatings and humiliation. The idea was to let the children sleep, and then I would wake each one of them and force them to drink the mixture. I would drink the rest and Sally would find us and report it. I lay on my bed and waited to hear snoring in the house. I lay on my bed crying all the time.

There was a bedside stool on which I put the radio. The only radio station, which I worked for, opened at six o'clock in the morning and closed at eleven o'clock. The God of heaven who judges the hearts of men had given me so much deep sleep that I left the radio on. It was the tone that was played when the station opened that woke me up, and it woke the children too. I hadn't executed my plan, and now it was too late. Tears had dried and caked on my face.

I tried to remember the events of the previous day, and it all came flooding back to me. I got out of bed and discarded the contents in the large jug. It was too late to do it. I wanted to appear as normal as possible, so I went to the kitchen to see if I could make breakfast for the children. The news bulletin came on the radio at seven o'clock. The first item was that of a man from my home village who had burned himself in a car with his four children. The youngest child was one year old like my Maxwell. The man had left a suicide note to explain that it was no accident, and that he wanted to die with all his children because he had been in an abusive relationship, and wouldn't stand leaving his children behind.

That incident hit me so hard that I imagined there would have been two stories of people who died with their innocent children. The story woke me up from my dream. I regretted having even thought about it, let alone planned it. I swore to never allow anybody to intimidate me. I vowed to park my car next to my enemy's. I promised myself that I would work hard for my boys to have a better life than they would have had with their father. I didn't know how I was going to do it because I was still so poor but I knew that God was going to make a way somehow.

CHAPTER 14

Pressing On

*Do not fear, I am with you; Do not be dismayed, For
I am your God. I will strengthen you so and help you;
I will uphold you with my righteous right hand.*
—*Isaiah 41:13*

At this point, I would like to inform those whose spouses die not to expect anything from family or friends. They will converge, cry with you a little, and then move on with their lives. Some friends will want to take advantage of the situation. A widow will appear to some people as a prospective mistress, what with the vulnerability and loneliness. Those who try to help will demand something in return. My case was worse, as I was still very young when my husband died. Although still in college, the job I was headed for was promising, so some people wanted to be associated with the fame that would come with the job. What saved me were my four young children who were too demanding for me to have thoughts about anything else.

As you will remember, when I came back to Nairobi after burying my husband, I was accompanied by my mother and mother-in-law, but my mother went back home at the end of two weeks. One of the reasons my mother went back earlier was that she was worried about my father, who didn't know how to cook.

My mother-in-law stuck with me for two months, but my sister-in-law Rachel forced her to go home. She accused me of turning her mother into a house help. That was just before we were thrown out of the Posta staff house. As usual, I didn't say anything but let my sister-in-law bundle her mother from my house to her own. Two days later, she put her on a bus to go back to the village—something she came to regret.

When my mother-in-law went back to the village, it was exactly as if she had walked straight into a live fire. My-father-in-law was not amused that she came with me to Nairobi and was always on my side. He also insinuated that we had squandered all the money from Daniel's death gratuity. He even accused my mother-in-law of having joined me in prostitution while in Nairobi. As if that wasn't enough, he became wild and threw everybody out of the home. Those who received the brunt of his wrath were my mother-in-law, who was beaten almost to the point of death, my brother-in-law Caleb (along with his wife Hellen and nine children), and my sister-in-law Jessica with her five children. This large family of four adults and fourteen children had nowhere to go but Nandi, where we had a farm without a house.

My mother-in-law and my sister-in-law occupied the tiny grass thatched mud hut that was left behind by the farm's former owner. Caleb and his wife sought sleeping places in neighbors' houses. Caleb was limping all the time, having been hit on the knee by his father, which hampered him from working on the farm for a while. When I visited them and saw the conditions in which they lived, I decided to put up a semi-permanent house, using the material we snatched from my father in law. It was large enough to accommodate Caleb with his family, with Jessica taking one of the bedrooms. My mother-in-law stayed in the little hut. The problem was how I could support them financially, when I had a problem making ends meet. My financial situation eased a little, though, when I was awarded a provisional house allowance of three hundred shillings, pending appointment to the designated job group.

Back home in Hamisi, Jacob, my father-in-law, collected all of his wife's belongings and burned them. He even uprooted the three hearth stones—a true abomination. It is taboo in Maragoli settings for one to burn clothes, set a house on fire, or remove the hearth stones. These acts require cleansing before the people can "eat together," meaning interact closely. Probably blinded by her deep hatred for me, my sister-in-law Rachel forced my mother-in-law to go back home without any cleansing or prayers to stop her from being turned into a supposed housemaid. My mother-in-law started becoming sickly as soon as she stepped back into her home. This may sound quaint and superstitious, but it's what I witnessed with my own eyes. She was carried to Kakamega Hospital, but all attempts to diagnose what was causing her bloated stomach and other symptoms were all futile. She died two weeks LATER, exactly ten months after the death of her favorite son, Daniel. Now I had no support in the family.

Being accused of taking the entire death gratuity was unfortunate. The fact is that I never got any money from the East Africa Posts and Communications, until after three years of hustling with my family. At that point, I got 27,000 shillings, an equivalent of $270. Having grown up in a strict moral setting, with M'ma insisting that we should never be greedy, I dished out the money to the family members. I gave Jacob ten thousand so he could share with his children, now that his wife was dead. He was not grateful at all. In fact, he told me the fact that I gave him ten thousand shillings means I kept hundreds of thousands.

My brother in law Zack even asked me for thirty thousand shillings to pay for the plot he was buying in Kakamega. Nobody believed that I didn't have the money. My children were starting to go to nursery schools, and since I wanted the best for them, I spent their father's gratuity on private nursery school tuition. This was St Joseph's Catholic Church school in Jericho, which was headed by Father Thomas. He treated children with kindness like his own. I must have made the right decision because my sons had a good start, although for primary education, they attended a public facility called Uhuru Primary School.

The first son to join Uhuru Primary School was Maxwell, the youngest of the four. Victor, Silvester, and Felix had earlier joined Harambee Primary School. This is a school in which I noticed tribalism of the highest degree. The head teacher grouped children from his ethnic group into one class, which he called Class A. All other tribes from the Nairobi cosmopolitan population were put in classes B and C. Because I was a celebrity, my children merited class B, but all the same, nothing happened in these two classes.

The children came home all the time saying they were just playing the whole day. I went to school to enquire what was going on. The answer was "Mrs. Erude, your children are foolish. We cannot waste time on children who are going nowhere. We have to concentrate on the bright ones." When I heard that, I didn't say anything to the headteacher. I simply walked to Uhuru, which had received the first-ever female headteacher from a different tribe in Nairobi. When I started explaining my case, she told me to stop because she knew what was going on.

Felgona Ndeda, for that was her name, told me to go right away, withdraw the children and bring them to Uhuru, which I immediately did. It didn't take a long time before my sons assumed first positions in that school. This head teacher was wonderful. She was later poached by President Moi and taken to his Moi Educational Center in Kibra. We were sad, but the replacement, Miss Kasidi was equally good. She was full of praises for me. I used to meet teachers who came for educational programs at the Voice of Kenya, and she would excitedly call out to me for introduction, saying "This is Mrs. Erude, a single parent but her sons at my school are so smart and disciplined" as the Harambee headteacher fidgeted. He was worried I would let the cat out of the bag.

Life with Sally as my housemate was not very easy, though. People may be friends, but when they live together, they will start noticing each other's shortcomings. Sally was the daughter of a preacher man, but she got pregnant out of wedlock, and her father disowned her. She got mad with the God of her father who allowed her to get pregnant. The Maragolis believe in prayer, and even when I wasn't going to church, they still came to the house to pray for me and the children. Sally would come screaming and pulling her daughter away from the living room, thus embarrassing the guests. She also always saw the mistakes my children made, never hers.

When I sat down with children to explain to them why they shouldn't repeat the mistake, she said that was not enough punishment. I spanked my children, but to her it wasn't enough—until I asked her if she wanted me to kill them for her to be satisfied. Another problem came from cleaning the kitchen. My house help was younger, and it took her longer to feed the many children.

Sally's house help was a woman who would feed only one child. She left the kitchen for my house help to clean every day. Sally would come to me accusing my maid of not being clean. I offered to clean the kitchen every day at midnight after work just to keep the peace. When accusations against my children and my maid became unbearable, I planned to take them home to my mother for a while, except Victor who was in nursery school at the time. They stayed in the village for three months, but I felt it was wrong for them to be that far. This is something I have lived to regret because the children suffered some allergies, which have left marks on their skin, especially Sylvester. I cried when I was told my youngest son, Maxwell, would cling to my sister who looked like me, in the same way Sylvester clung to Zack when Daniel died.

On the other hand, Sally was a good friend. We were inseparable. We did shifts together, especially night shifts. We shopped together. We had the same friends and foes. Anybody who attacked one of us had attacked both of us. And most of the time, when I cried for Daniel, Sally was there to listen to me, providing a much-needed shoulder. In fact, she blurted out one statement that's seen me through life. She said, "Imagine, Gladys, you might come to have a very bright future." That statement gave me hope. But sometimes that hope could not survive the onslaught of life. The day I almost killed my own children and took my own life is an example of that. After coming back to my senses, I got onto my knees and thanked God for the deep sleep that had prevented me from doing the unthinkable.

Although I prayed all the time, I couldn't go to church. I had to hide to pray because Sally didn't like prayers. It wasn't until I read a verse in the Bible, in which Jesus says "whoever is ashamed of me, I will be ashamed of him before my father." I decided to never be ashamed of my salvation at all. New Year's Eve of 1977, a neighbor invited me to an overnight prayer meeting. There, I found people so happy and rejoicing in the Lord. I thought "who am I to reject God?" I was just a drop in the ocean. If I couldn't beat them at their game, I should join them. I gave my life to Christ once again and from that time, I have never been ashamed of Him. I became a regular church member.

CHAPTER 15

Work and Moving on

Let your eyes look directly forward, and your gaze be straight before you. Ponder the path of your feet; then all your ways will be sure. Do not swerve to the right or to the left; turn your foot away from evil.
—*Proverbs 4: 25-27*

Our graduation from the Kenya Institute of Mass Communication was at the end of March 1976. A man called Stanley came to represent the director of broadcasting. He kept leering lecherously at me, which I found very uncomfortable. I was still living on edge due to the death of my husband, and all that followed was still very fresh in my mind. I later came to learn that Stanley was the head of Radio Traffic, which was the section that handled all the transmitted material, from programs to commercials and announcements. He was from a certain ethnic group and the head of the Swahili service Benson, also came from this community. To make matters worse, the head of the English service, Oscar, belonged to the community as well.

My friend Sally was then at an outright advantage because she just happened to come from the very same ethnic group. I, however, was disadvantaged as an "outsider."

Other people were assigned duties, but I wasn't. After about six months, I decided to initiate my own program. The program would be aired twice. The third week, I would go to the studio ready to record my program, which was beginning to gain momentum, only to find another producer, usually Sally, having been secretly assigned as my personal initiative. This happened several times until I gave up. Since my meager salary was still coming, I wouldn't bother working. For two years I didn't do anything at the Voice of Kenya, and nobody seemed to worry. It didn't click that I had to do certain things to be accepted. I remained a sworn enemy of Stanley all my working days. I was happy when he retired, but I had made other enemies who took over for him. It looked like he told them to keep an eye on me. One such person was Francis.

In 1978, I went home to visit my mother and sister. I was trying to explain to my sister how a Luo man called Olocho had helped me to complete my course at KIMC. My sister asked, "Who?" and when I repeated the name, she pointed to a large house on a hill in Vihiga and told me, "That's his house. He is not a Luo." All those times David Olocho helped me, we never spoke any other language apart from English. As it turned out, he was my sister's neighbor, and they worshipped in the same Quaker church together. When they met in the church one Sunday, my sister Selina thanked him for helping her "widowed sister" and he also asked who the sister was. He believed I was a Luo too because of the name Erude, as *rude* means "twins" in the Luo language.

I also learned that Olocho is a Luo expression meaning "he or she has won."

In the same year, Inzoberi John, a retired Veteran broadcaster came back to Voice of Kenya and served as the head of Swahili service. Olocho, who knew him well, wanted to know how I was doing. Inzoberi discovered that I wasn't working at all but drawing a salary for nothing. He called me to the office and wanted to know what was happening. He immediately ordered that I be put on the continuity roster. Continuity duties are what are known as transmission. To be in studio to transmit recorded material, tell time, play music and transmit commercials. I was also voice tested for news reading and found it fit. All of a sudden, all the local dailies were talking of a new announcer who played the best music. This was after I went through some challenges of being almost the only non-coastal person, born and bred in the interior of Kenya to have anything to do with continuity on the Swahili service. Those who were there like Obege, Abila, and Akinyi had either been raised in Mombasa or Dar es Salaam. I fought the rejection and won.

In 1979, Margaret Mwalagho, who had produced the women's program called *Akina Mama* was transferred to Mombasa. This program was given to me. Everybody expected it to die because they were used to hearing Margaret. I wanted to refuse, but I took it and changed the sig-tune. If somebody wanted me to fail by giving me a veteran's production, they did the opposite. This program opened a lot of doors for me. This was a time when women all over the world were beginning to realize their rights and rightful place in society. It made me attend many seminars and meetings, where allowances were paid. I never knew such things happened. I was therefore happy that I could make a little more on the side to feed my family.

In January of 1980, I was accepted at the Radio Netherlands Training Centre. Eight people had been interviewed for this training, but I was selected. This was the beginning of such trainings and my sojourns in several counties of the world, like France, Belgium, Zimbabwe, Mauritius, Madagascar, and Germany. To crown it all, I attended and covered the 4th UN Conference on Women in Beijing, China. On our way to China, the Kenyan delegation decided to spend two days in Dubai.

Apart from the duties listed above, I used to do live broadcasts especially during agricultural trade fairs at showgrounds.

In due course, The Voice of Kenya was changed to Kenya broadcasting Corporation in 1991. As a state corporation, we had to make our own revenue apart from the government subsidy. On our path to stability, we passed through different directors. We hardly realized any physical changes, except when one of them built a wall around it and claimed it cost fourteen million, when we, the workers, still earned peanuts. Real change occurred when we got Mr. Philip Okundi, who raised our salaries and improved working conditions... from my personal viewpoint, that is.

Okundi allowed the producers to act as marketers, which meant looking out for program sponsorship, and getting a twenty-percent commission from the deal. I grabbed the chance and worked hard to get sponsors for my programs. Trouble came when I didn't share my commissions with my bosses. I became the target, sometimes of blatant lies.

I used to go home every week when my sister became terminally ill. She had lost her husband, and I had to do all I could to make her final days on earth as painless as possible. I always traveled from Kisumu by Wepesi, a Peugeot service company. They knew me, and they would drop me off at the gate. One Monday, I went to the studio to leave my bag, and then walked to the office of my boss, Francis, to make a call to my house in Nairobi to inform the children that I had arrived and was at work. Francis welcomed me to the office and left, telling me to make as many calls as I wanted. Remember, we didn't have cell phones then. I innocently made one call to my house and sat there waiting for Francis because he told me not to leave his office unattended. He came back after thirty minutes. I thanked him for the call, and we even joked about me having tested the seat of the boss.

I was therefore surprised the following day when I met my Radio Programs Manager, Eulalia, who was so mad at me. She ordered me to go to her office in which she screamed at me for leading a group of Luhyas to finish Francis. Because I didn't know what she was talking about, I let her yell. She finished by throwing a pen on the table and wanted to know why I went to Francis's office to attack him with a knife. Apparently, when Francis left me in his office, he had gone to report me to the Managing Director. The MD, in turn, turned to Eulalia. After I explained the case to her, she was shocked. She immediately wrote a letter to Francis asking him to explain why he had lied. Since no action was taken against Francis, I brought up the matter in a staff meeting of all radio staff members. That spelled doom for me. I became a gold fish which has no hiding place, especially when Francis became the Radio Programs Manager, after Eulalia went to UNICEF.

Our animosity continued until we received a new MD, who listened to his lies and acted upon them. Together with a man who took over the radio traffic, Joash, they made sure they formed lies against me. They reported me to the MD Khamis, who didn't give me a chance to defend myself, but had the disciplinary committee recommend that I be sent away. I had worked so hard for the corporation, but nobody appreciated me. There was a law that one could only merit pension after serving the corporation for ten years. I had three months to get there. I pleaded, I cried, and I begged to no avail. Surprisingly, the people retrenched at the time were those who didn't agree with Francis.

We were nine from radio: seven Luhyas, one Kikuyu, a pastor who didn't subscribe to the tribalistic *uthamak'i* ideology, and one Kisii. I went to see Musalia Mudavadi, then the Minister for Transport and Communications, three times to help us, but I guess he had better things to do. Lastly, I went to the permanent secretary, who was Titus Naikuni at the time. He was the only person who felt that I had been treated unfairly. He immediately wrote a letter to Khamis, instructing him to give me a hearing. Unfortunately, as I waited for a bus near a kiosk to go back to town after the meeting with Naikuni, I heard on radio that Titus Naikuni had been relieved of his duties as permanent secretary for transport and communications. He was replaced by Muthaura, a Kikuyu, and I knew my case would not go anywhere. I accepted and moved on.

I decided to register my own advertising agency and sourced for sponsorship. The companies would pay me for production, and KBC gave me twenty percent of every production I gave them. I realized that when God is pushing you out of a situation, He always has better plans for you. Unfortunately, Francis did not live to see my prosperity. He was retired two weeks after me. The letter of retirement shocked him so much that he passed away. I did not rejoice; I would have loved to have closure with him, but that was God's will. Joash, on the other hand, carried all the retribution. He too was retired but first had to move out of a corporation house before he could receive his dues. Six months after, I met him in town looking sick and bought him lunch.

CHAPTER 16

The walk with Christ

But seek first the kingdom of God and his righteousness, and all these things will be added to you.
—Matthew 6:33

I have stated before that I grew up in an environment of strict Quaker morals, right from Sunday school days, with my mother who deeply feared sin and hellfire, and M'ma who was my early childhood instructor, of course not forgetting Rosa, the Sunday school teacher. Quaker church services are called meetings.

There were village meetings, and then several village meetings used to come together for bi-weekly meetings. In this case, village meetings converged on Sunday mornings twice a month for the "Fifteen." Several Fifteen meetings made up a monthly meeting. All the fifteen meetings converged once a month for the monthly meeting. Next was a quarterly meeting, which was held in Munzatsi. We walked seven miles to go to the quarterly meeting, which met once every three months. The yearly meeting was held at Kaimosi

Friends Mission, before they decentralized into other yearly meetings.

The yearly meetings were in charge of organizing Christmas carols, choosing the songs and the verses for monthly meetings to compete in reciting. At the Tigoi monthly meeting, the elders honored high school students by singing songs in English, calling it "the language that had finished their cows," which meant parents had to sell cows to pay tuition in high school boarding. Every primary pupil dreamt of working hard in school so as to join the group in the future.

In 1962 when I was a standard five pupil, I became an associate member of the Friends Church, or a "Christian of the first book.". One had to be taught in class and be given Bible verses to cram and recite in an interview-like questioning session. After all was done, the candidates came together for the final swearing or graduation ceremony. A village elder would then ask questions like, "Will you stop drinking alcohol and cigarettes?"

The candidates answered, "Yes," in unison, except one question which was, "Will you stop having anything to do with boys or girls?" Here, some answered yes while others kept quiet because most of them were young boys and girls, and they weren't sure that they would be able to keep such a promise. It wasn't until 1965, while I was in class eight, that I studied to be a full member, or "the second book." It was tougher than the first, but I passed. By the time I went to high school in 1965, I was a very good Christian and very active in the youth ministry. I encountered a completely different type of life in high school, though.

As much of a good Christian and member of the Christian union as I was, I was a member of drama club, debate, and choir too. I was the best dancer during our entertainment sessions. Life was good. We were fearful of the woman who stood at the gate every Sunday as we entered the church to press our bellies to see if we were pregnant, or checked our fingers to see if we had painted our nails, pulling earrings from the ears of those who dared to wear them. That did not prevent us from being the fun-loving young people just the same.

When I got married, or rather when I took my son at Hamisi for baptism, I discovered that my new family went to the Pentecostal Assemblies of God Church, which was a charismatic church in which people clapped hands while singing and danced, which was forbidden in the Quaker church. I found it hard to start clapping my hands, and it took me time to adjust. At the same time, I was used to silent prayers in my home church, but now I had to get used to loud prayers and shouts as the devil was ordered to leave. I have since come to love it so much that I could scarcely give it up for anything.

The first church I went to in Nairobi was Dr. Aggrey PAG Church. There were two people who never listened to anything that was preached because they were wailing and rolling on the ground in the throes of "The Holy Spirit," which totally put me off. I therefore went to East Leigh PAG. Here, the pastor was an old man who was down to earth. I convinced my husband to join me, and so we became members for a while before he died. We sang in the choir together, our choirmaster being Solomon Mulema.

It was after my husband's death that I realized church members were human beings. I didn't like the way they treated me like something that was there for grabs. I expected them to be compassionate and understanding, but I got the impression that some of the men had ulterior motives. The wives were hawk-eyed, trying to see whether I would greet their husbands in a particular way that would suggest something. I knew I was alone. That's when I quit the church and stayed home for two years. I didn't even want prayers because I knew that if any man came to pray for me, he would be after something else, and then the wife would come to confront me.

On New Year's Eve of 1978, my neighbor Joyce Vuhura invited me to an overnight vigil. Her church had been founded by the famous gospel musicians Isaya Symekher and Mary Atieno, and it was called International Fellowship Church Jericho. When I entered the room, although it was cold outside, I felt like there was fire in the room. People were praising in earnest and looked very happy. I enjoyed the whole service and decided to quit being angry with God. He didn't need me because He had all these people. I wasn't going to beat them, so I joined them. When the altar call was made after the preaching, I was the first to walk to the front, to rededicate my life to Jesus. It was like a heavy stone had been lifted from my shoulders.

When Sunday came, I went to Uhuru PAG church to announce my membership, and they were happy to receive me. I joined their choir, and after a short while, I was made the chairlady for the choir. I sourced for places to perform, so the choir could have its own kitty. But as soon as we brought the money, the church elders would want it to divide among themselves. I became very vocal and told them off. Uhuru was still a village, so we used to go to Makadara PAG for the bigger assembly.

The Pastor there was a down-to-earth spirit-filled man of God called Caleb Ogutu. He served there until he was transferred to Dandora, as we received Elkanah Salamba, another knowledgeable pastor. He was a well-liked pastor, and as it were, his wife Ruth had been born and bred in Uhuru Church. We went to great heights under Salamba, until he was transferred to Westland, as they brought us the pastor who used to serve there. This was an older pastor who believed if one didn't cry and roll on the ground, speaking in tongues, then he or she wasn't Christian enough.

I was a well-known person, a celebrity if you like, because I worked at a radio station and almost everybody knew who I was. The people I knew in Westlands started coming to tell me how this pastor would visit the former members of his congregation and talk about the members at Makadara. He once told them that, "If the likes of Erude thinks her money will take her to heaven without speaking in tongues, I will throw them out of my church." I did not take it lightly. I met him at Uhuru shopping Centre and screamed at him, but he didn't utter a word. Then I felt very bad for behaving like a fool. I was haunted by my behavior until I looked for him and apologized, gave him some money, at which point he prayed for me. He said, "May your doors be opened".

The following week, I was promoted after mark-timing for fourteen years. Another promotion followed after three months. The same year, I was voted presenter of the year and received an award. As if that was not enough, Family Planning

Association of Kenya selected me to attend a symposium on soap opera writing in Harare, Zimbabwe. I understood why God tags forgiveness to Christianity.

It was during this pastor's tenure at the Makadara Assembly that the church split into two. Some people went to form the Buru Buru Assembly's PAG while others who agreed with the pastor stayed on. I was among those who went to BuruBuru. At Buru Buru, I was made the Sunday school superintendent. I served in that capacity for a while, until I was made the treasurer for the women's division. I wasn't actually appointed, but I took the position by force because the women's leader wanted to be alone in the office without a treasurer—probably so she could misappropriate church funds. Many women feared working with her, but I practically imposed myself into the position.

I served in that capacity for two years, and then I became the secretary. I was in Mauritius attending a Radio production course when our pastor was transferred, but those who rejected him quit the church, including the director of women's services. On my coming back, I was informed that I would head the women's department. I didn't like it. It took the new pastor and members many days to convince me to accept it. I prayed about it and found peace and liberty to assume the role. I held that position for eight years. Many people tried to fight me, but I would be re-elected every two years.

My problem was my inability to stomach some things the church leaders were doing. For instance, when we were asked to give money to buy nice seats for the District overseer, I would ask what difference there was between us and the biblical tax collectors. There were seventy-two assemblies that made up the Bahati District. Every assembly gave ten percent of the total tithe and offerings. That would amount to thousands of shillings, which was the overseer's salary. We still had to contribute to buy tires and fuel for his car, and every female director also gave some money for his food. I said I would do it if KBC was giving me money on top of my salary for food. That did not go well with the district leaders, and they started planning to eliminate me. Luckily enough, I had a mole in that committee who told me everything. I would have gone ahead and defied their plans in every way, but God made me sick. After hospitalization, I had a restricted diet of no sugar, no salt, and no soft drinks.

More trouble came when I vied for the district women's leader. The district overseer did not hide the fact that I was a widow, and the Bible forbids widows to lead. They rigged me out. I didn't talk to him for a long time, but his wife died only two days after I met him and shook his hand. It reminded me of Exodus 22:22-23.

CHAPTER 17

God's Grace

*Count it all joy, my brothers, when you meet
trials of various kinds, for you know that the
testing of your faith produces steadfastness. And
let steadfastness have its full effect, that you may
be perfect and complete, lacking in nothing.*
—James 1:2-4

That I am still alive to tell this story is by the grace of God. Apart from my childhood trauma in the hands of my Aunt Lily, and the mistreatment by my family-in-law, there are other things that happened in my life that nearly ended it.

I have mentioned that it was when Inzoberi John came back to work for *Voice of Kenya* that I was noticed and assigned jobs. The first thing he did was assign to me a program on the international news, *The World This Week*, or *Dunia Wiki Hii* as it was known in Kiswahili. For a long time, I co-presented the program with him and the controller of programs, Hassan Mazoa. It was a very popular program, and together with continuity duties, made me popular too. I was also assigned the children's program that used to be presented by Dolly Achieng' Shikuku, who had been transferred to Kakamega. I initiated a gospel request program too, which gained a large following from Tanzania because of the music I played.

Much later, Inzoberi left VoK and went to work with Family Planning Association of Kenya as a Communication and Education Coordinator. One of his duties was to produce a fifteen-minute weekly program to teach Kenyans the importance of spacing children and having smaller families that they could manage better. Since he was busy traveling all over the world, he commissioned me to take care of the *Panga Uzazi* program. I enjoyed doing it so much that I came to learn and have family planning information at my fingertips. I became a senior volunteer in the association and even rose to the position of secretary/treasurer in the Nairobi branch.

I thought it wise to preach the gospel of family planning wherever I went and in whatever I did. I explained it quietly to women who feared it, thinking they would be sick. Some thought their husbands would leave them. The biggest lie about family planning was that women would lose their libido and that their husbands would marry other wives. I taught them otherwise.

Our main sponsor was John Hopkin's University in the US, and Planned Parenthood International. Apart from spacing children, they brought us knowledge on how to screen some diseases like cancer through a Pap Smear. This is a test that needed to be taken every year by women from sixteen years of age to forty-nine. The tests were paid for but needed a woman to pay a registration fee of fifty shillings, the equivalent of fifty cents. I would get hold of women and take them to our clinics for testing. I paid from my pocket for those who didn't have any money.

The nurses at all the clinics were my friends, so one day they asked me why I don't take time to be tested too. It occurred to me that I was doing other people's work, but mine was not being done. Immediately, I went in for specimen taking. It took two weeks for the results to be known. When my results were out, every nurse and every officer was looking for me. I went to the clinic and was given a letter to take to Kenyatta Hospital. They insisted that it was urgent but because I was not in pain, I took my time. The letter was in my purse for a month. When I met one of my nurse friends, she asked what the doctor said. I told her I had not even gone to Kenyatta Hospital, and she reprimanded me like a child. Even then, I didn't do anything.

The daughter of our deacon had surgery at Kenyatta Hospital, and per the custom, many church members were visiting her in the hospital. One of the women leaders in our church, Priscilla, was a nurse at Kenyatta. She used to assist many people in going to see doctors or simply getting appointments. The queues were too long at the hospital, and patients used to line up a whole day without being seen. Some died while still queuing for medical attention. So, after seeing the deacon's daughter and praying for her, Priscilla was seeing us off when I remembered the letter in my purse. I called her back when she was going back to the hospital and showed her the letter, asking what it meant because I could not understand the medical terminology. She was visibly startled when she read the date of the letter. I had had it for six weeks. She said, "We have to go back to the hospital." I watched her instruct people to open a file for me and fix an appointment with immediate effect.

When I went to see the doctor after three days, he pronounced that I had cancer of the stomach and it was in the third stage. When I jumped, he yelled at me and I bolted out of the room. I went to see another doctor who explained to me that according to the records, I indeed had cancer and it was at the third stage, but if immediate and swift action was taken, I could be saved. It took me three weeks to find a bed at Kenyatta national Hospital.

I was admitted to ward five of women surgical cases which was the cleanest ward in the hospital. Surgery took place only on Wednesdays; those who missed had to wait for another Wednesday. Women had been residing there for a period of one to two years, waiting for surgery. Those who missed surgery could go home and come back on Monday morning for the doctor's rounds to determine who would be on the list for the following Wednesday. It therefore took me three months to get the surgery. September 14, 1990, was my lucky day. I was woken up at four o'clock in the morning to get ready for surgery and later wheeled into the theatre at seven o'clock. I didn't come to until four o'clock. The doctor told me they had given up on me but I woke up when they were thinking of calling in the mortuary attendants. I didn't know all that because all the time they had seen me as unconscious, I was in a very serene place. I was resting peacefully when I heard a beautiful choir singing a hymn from *Songs of Praise* called "Glory to His Name." I wanted to sing along, but I couldn't remember the words. Then, I saw the brown hairy hands of a man handing me a hymn book. I was so happy, but when I opened my mouth to sing, somebody woke me up. To my surprise, the doctors and nurses who had surrounded me broke into applause, I looked around at them, and then I sank back into a deep sleep.

They say the devil is a liar—a stubborn, adamant one at that. Perhaps that is why members of my church had to yell and scream at him. In 1996, I lost my voice completely for a year, which was very distressing, seeing as I was a broadcaster and I needed my voice. The stomach cancer had gone into recession after the treatment, but now it had metastasized to the throat. I didn't think of it in those terms, until I tried everything in vain. At least at this time, I could afford a better hospital. I went to Nairobi Hospital, but the clerk referred me to another doctor in Hurlingham.

My sons, Sly, Felix, and Max, drove me to the doctor. She did some tests and concluded that, indeed, the cancer had spread to my throat. She scheduled a day for surgery, but I left the doctor's office crying. I didn't go for the surgery; instead, my friend called Ruth Martha Namai, who came to my house and said she dreamed about praying for me. This is a lady I met at Kilimambogo Teacher's College and had become as close to as a sister, though we didn't meet often. She had been cured of cancer three times through prayer. When she came to my house, she found that I could not speak. At work, I had resorted to production, although my favorite was presentation.

Ruth started praying at the door. She prayed and cried to the Lord to heal me and restore my job. I was convinced that God had heard my prayer and that he would answer me. Three days after that prayer, I woke up and my voice had been restored. If that's not a miracle, I don't know what is.

In 1984, I was dressing up to go to a funeral where my colleague had lost a four-year-old son. Suddenly I was breathless. My heart started pounding heavily in my chest. I wasn't even able to call one of my sons to come to my rescue. I tried to lie down, but that did not help. This went on for about fifteen minutes and stopped as abruptly as it had started, leaving me very shaky with a dry mouth. I didn't know what it was, but it happened again after six months and later started happening more often.

Every time I got that attack, I went to the doctor but by then I would be ok. No doctor seemed to understand what was ailing me. Three years down the line, I went to see another doctor called Shiraz. He told me that those were heart palpitations that could cause a heart attack. I didn't follow it up, although I could have been easily put in the same group with epileptic people. Several times I had attacks in the middle of town and I would be surrounded by people, and sometimes carried to the hospital. But by the time I arrived at the hospital, they would have stopped. I almost believed in witchcraft and probably would have if it weren't for my staunch Christian upbringing.

Some people advised me to lose weight. I enrolled in a gym and was gaining ground when I tried aerobics and put a strain on the heart. That day, I had eight attacks in one day, although it used to take between four to six months to get an attack again. I remember getting an attack while I was on air reading news. I remained quiet for a while, and then continued when it stopped. The day I had eight attacks, I was in town on business, having given my son our car to take it for service as we intended to travel to the village in two days' time. No sooner had my son left than I had the eighth attack.

I sat down on the pavement in the street and called for a taxi. I remember that was in 2002 when we were gearing up for elections that gave us a little reprieve as far as democracy is concerned. When the taxi man came, he helped me to the car and asked me where I wanted to go. I told him to just drive to any hospital. He took me to Mater Hospital.

I went through the usual admission procedure like registration but by the time I saw the doctor, the palpitations had stopped. The doctor told me to go home because I wasn't sick, but I refused to go, and luckily enough, I had the ninth attack in her office. She jumped and got scared. She called in other doctors, but they all said they had never seen a heart race so fast. They wanted to admit me on condition that I pay fifty thousand upfront. I didn't have the money on me but I had an insurance card, which they declined to accept. They asked to transfer me to another hospital where the card could be accepted. I chose Nairobi Hospital. I called my son to pick me up from Mater and take me home. When he came, he insisted we go to Nairobi Hospital first.

At Nairobi Hospital, I gave them the test reports from Matter Hospital. They tried to test my blood again and looked at the ECG graph from Mater but said I wasn't sick. I went crazy and said I needed to see a cardiologist. They called Dr. Kariuki, who came within ten minutes. He asked me to lie on a hospital bed, and the moment he touched me to examine me, I had a tenth attack. He reprimanded the clerks for even thinking I wasn't sick. I was admitted straight to the high dependency unit for fifteen days. During this time, Dr Kariuki did not leave any stone unturned in my body. He discovered that I had been asthmatic all along, but since I wasn't on medication, my lungs had put pressure on my heart. Together with Dr Silverstein, they did what they call catheterization, which is a type of heart surgery but not open-heart. He put me on blood thinners and high blood pressure control medicine, and above all, an asthma inhaler that I use when needed. After one year, I stopped taking blood thinners, but once in a while, I used the inhaler. God had saved me again.

In 2004, I visited my sons in the US. I had earlier noticed a swelling in my gums that was increasing in size every day. I couldn't go to a doctor because I was not a resident of the US and so I didn't have hospital insurance. Surprisingly, a friend by the name of Miriam Kisia came to see me and told me that her dentist had rolled out promotional consultancy for people who didn't have insurance. For two weeks, he charged only one dollar for consultation. He took tests of the swelling, and the result revealed that it was cancer. I started crying because my sister had died of the same gum cancer two years before. He reassured me that all would be fine because it was early enough to use what he called 'local chemo.' He intended to give me treatment once a week for five weeks, but I had only three weeks more to stay in The States before my time to go back to Kenya came. The swelling went down and I haven't had another welling of that sort. All glory and honor to God who heals.

CHAPTER 18

Still it blossoms.

I will go before you and make the rough places smooth; I will shatter the doors of bronze and cut through their iron bars.
—Isaiah 45:2

It seems to me that a lot of things in my life came to be, despite prodigious obstacles. God has always leveled mountains and filled up valleys along my way. I have been like a flower that has flourished and bloomed in every soil that I have found myself in. No one teaches a flower how to bloom; it's in its nature to blossom because that is what God created it to do. No matter what circumstances it is subjected to, it blossoms still. None of the challenges I have experienced have stopped my destiny or God's purpose in my life.

In January of 1980, I went to the Netherlands for Radio Production Training. My letter was dated November 14, 1979. I didn't know about it until January 10, 1980. One or two of the bosses sat on the letter so that by the time they gave it to me, it would be too late to process my papers.

That was a Friday, so I decided I would not go. Before that, I talked to my boss, Jim Akenga, who encouraged me to try and obtain the necessary papers and go. He told me that I needed a birth certificate, a passport, a visa, and clearance from Directorate of Personnel Management. I just gave up.

On Sunday when I went to church, I told Pastor Ogutu that I was to travel abroad for training, but it was too late. He said we needed to pray about it and that God would open ways for me to get papers in good time. He prayed, and then called my cousin Rajab Mwondi, who attended the same church with me. He told him that I needed help. Then he called our church treasurer, Meshack, who worked with Kenya Airways. He asked him to please help me get the necessary papers. The pastor deemed it a chance of a lifetime which I shouldn't miss.

Meshack said he was on leave and thus had time to help. He also said that he knew some people who could help. The following day, which was a Monday, he came to my house very early and took me to Sheria House to apply for a birth certificate. We went to somebody called Kitungulu, who filled out the forms while we waited and gave us the receipts after we paid the requisite ten shillings. He said that we could use the receipts to apply for a passport. We walked across to the passport place and met a man called Odera, whom Meshack knew. Odera accepted the receipts to process the passport but said we would need the real certificate to pick it up. He dropped me back at Broadcasting House as he went home. He came back the following day, picked me up, and took me to receive the birth certificate and passport. I then went to Uchumi House, which housed the Royal Netherlands

Embassy, and applied for a visa. They told me to pick it up on a Friday.

Meanwhile, I went to Broadcasting House to apply for imprest and write a letter to the DPM. At the DPM, I was lucky enough to meet Grace Wakhungu, who was the lady in yellow at my interview at the Kenya Institute of Mass Communication. She still recalled me, as I was wearing a yellow dress as well, coincidentally. Grace had a love, and you can guess what color her car, a beetle, was. She processed my clearance as I waited, and she wished me well.

Meshack came to my house on Friday morning and took me to pick my visa, and then I went to get my yellow fever shot at the Nairobi City Council Offices. The last thing he did for me was to get me into the bank on a Saturday morning to sign my traveler's cheques. He took me home and promised to come later in the evening with the Pastor and his wife for prayers because my flight was on Sunday morning. My church elders came that evening, and Meshack's wife, who was my close friend, was the one serving the guests. I had to retrieve my mother to come from the village to care for my children for six months. My church deacons came too.

The following day, the last time for Meshack to render his help, he was there with his car and his wife. My cousin Mwondi brought his car too. Then I had the work transport vehicle to take me to the airport. Meshack was an aircraft officer with Kenya Airways, so he was allowed to take me to the flight, together with my mother. Everybody else remained outside. I was *very* grateful to everyone who helped make this trip a success.

We exchanged letters with Meshack and the wife all the time I was in Hilversum, Netherlands. I believed we were family friends, but when I came back, I found a funny story. Apparently, whoever saw me with Meshack chasing my travel documents concluded that we were lovers and had broadcast it to everybody who cared to listen. Meshack and his wife never had children and people concluded on their own that we had agreed to get married because I was a widow who could get babies while his wife couldn't.

I was so distraught that I cried and used all means to refute those claims. I went to see Aggy, Meshack's wife, and ask her if she had heard the rumor. She asked me if that was the first rumor I was being implicated in because she didn't care at all. She even mentioned one of my church deacons, who was a driver at Kenya airways, and how this deacon had gone to her house to report the case to her. She said she knew what I was doing with her husband. This infuriated the deacon so much that he went trumpeting to everybody how single women are home breakers. All through that, I knew I was innocent.

Long after I'd had my boys Tony and Byron, people concluded that Meshack was the father. Sometime later, there was a fire incident at Meshack and Aggy's house, which claimed Aggy's life and left Meshack with burns all over his body. The rumor was that I was the cause of the fire because I had taken my two boys to that house and asked Aggy to leave. I just don't know how people sit down to fabricate a story and make it spread like wildfire, but then again, they say a falsehood can travel around the world in the time it takes the truth to put on its shoes. The thing is that nobody has ever known the cause of the fire, and I was really sad to have lost my friend. To prove my innocence, I participated fully in the funeral and even went home for burial. If that rumor died down, any rumor can die.

Being single has a lot of disadvantages. You are blamed for things you don't even do. Another rumor that devastated me was about the Godfather to my children. During a Pentecostal baptism, one has to have somebody to carry his clothes for change after the immersion in the water. That person is the Godfather, and this individual was very close to us. He was the treasurer of the church in Buru Buru, and we sort of had the same vision for the church. When I supported what he said, his enemies decided that I supported him because we had something going on between us.

The rumor became worse when I asked him to find an attachment job in IT for my son Maxwell because he was the head of IT in his organization. He did exactly that, but instead of field attachment, which many people call internship, he asked his bosses to employ him because he was a good worker. I was very happy. The same year, I went to China to cover the 4th UN Conference on Women in Beijing China. The Kenyan delegation spent three days in Dubai, and I took the chance to buy something to thank my sons' Godfather with. I bought him a watch, and a very nice fabric material for making a dress for the wife. In Kenya, we have seamstresses all over who make something the way you want it.

When I came back from China, I called the man to tell him I had arrived and I had something for him and his wife. He said they would come for it. When they came to my house later that evening, the wife had changed. She wasn't the same friend I had before I went to China.

I later discovered that a certain woman who wanted her daughter employed did not get the chance my son had, so she had started a rumor that I was more than a friend to my sons' Godfather, which his wife believed. I tried to explain, deny, and cry to no avail. The wife even threatened to crush me with her car. I was innocent, but nobody would believe me. I was lucky to have known what the wife did on the side because she was my friend. To put a stop to this stupid rumor, I threatened to tell everybody that she was the cheater. I even recorded her conversation with my colleague with whom she cheated on the husband. The matter died shortly thereafter.

Perhaps the worst blame was that of the death of my brother Jairus, who was the son of my other mother. We were very close because we had grown up together, and he was two years older than me. When my husband died, he took it upon himself to stand in the gap for the children, taking them places.

My brother worked with the Ministry of Lands as a draftsman. He married on the December 30 of 1978. He had his annual leave in April of 1979, so he and his wife, Joyce, went to the village to spend the leave. He had applied to the Public Service Commission for a promotion. His interview came in the middle of his break, and so he had to leave his wife home as he came back to Nairobi for the interview. After the interview, he told me he still had a week and he would rather go back home to be with his wife. He was supposed to resume duty in May of that year. He left home on Sunday morning aboard a Bus Union. He didn't arrive in Nairobi.

After a week, we were wondering why he wasn't coming to work. His cousin came to Nairobi with his medicinal herbs because he used to get bouts of nose bleeding, but with the herbs, they weren't so frequent. That cousin was the one who told us that he left home a week ago. We started the search in all hospitals, police stations, and mortuaries. We later got news that there had been an accident in Molo where many people died and survivors were in hospitals in Nakuru and Molo. We started with Molo but didn't find him. The body was lying in Nakuru Provincial General Hospital mortuary, with his ID card still in his pocket but the money he had was gone. The police were only interested in the money but not the ID card.

We carried the body to Nairobi, where the bulk of his friends were, to make funeral arrangements. By the time we buried my brother, my stepmother and her sisters had started a rumor that I was the one who visited a witch doctor and asked him to kill my brother. They did not specify the motive but there the story went. At first, my sisters, Mary, and Dorcas were not party to it but were later convinced that my mother and I had caused my brother's death.

The only person who remained neutral was Laban. The story then was picked up by my uncle Peter and his wife, and we became enemies for a while. Things became worse when I went to Europe. They found a motive in that. They started claiming that I killed my brother so I could take his place to go abroad. I cried for a while, then decided I had heard too much in my short life. I wasn't even working with my brother in the same organization. How could I have exchanged places? For a long time, the other side of the family did not talk to us, up until the death of our father reunited us.

I have since realized that nobody just dies in the Luhya community, especially the Maragoli. "Somebody" causes deaths, even when they occur in road accidents. I ceased to care as long as I know that God sees and knows the truth. And that is what I have decided to firmly found myself upon; what I always live by. I have fully realized that the solid rock upon which I am established will always be my strength as long as I live.

I have always tried to strive to excel where my detractors did not reach. If anybody looked down on me because they had what I did not, I made sure I acquired mine too. My motto was to park my car next to my enemy's.

A literal example of this is when Patrick, who helped my son go to America, was coming home; I went to meet him at the airport together with my cousin, whose children he had helped too. I was with my son Sylvester, and we could have taken a taxi home. But my cousin, who had several cars, implored us to go to his house, eat with our visitor, and then he would drive us home. As usual, there was a blackout, and the phone in my house didn't work without electricity. It was at the beginning of digital phones before cell phones. I kept asking my cousin to take us home but it fell on deaf ears. At three o'clock in the morning, he said he was too tired to go to Kariobangi South from Nairobi South C. His mother, a friend of my late mother, said, "My child cannot go to such places at night. He might lose his car to thugs."

There was a couple from Buru Buru, which is nearer my house. I asked the couple to give us a ride, but the woman, who was the breadwinner because the husband had lost his job, said, "You can spend the night at our house and take the bus tomorrow." When the husband heard that, he took the wheel and told us to get into the car. He went via town and Kasarani and took us home. He told the wife, "Never treat people like that. I wanted to show you that I used to drink and come home when I had money and nobody took the car from me." I was so grateful to the man. The following day, I emptied my bank account and bought a car. As we talk now, the woman has been reduced to no more than a street urchin, yet she used to be a banker. It's unfortunate that the good husband died. I have made it my life's motto to take it as a challenge when someone flaunts something I don't have in my face, to not rest until I have it too.

CHAPTER 19

The Race is Run

*Be strong and courageous . . . Do not be discouraged,
for the Lord your God will be with you wherever you go.
—Joshua 1:9*

Raising my children was the toughest race I have ever run. I didn't have much when they were young. We suffered depravity at times, but what we had in our house was laughter. There was no hatred; even the boys who used to fight when they were younger just like any other family eventually stopped and have always been there for one another.

The challenges of juggling life as a single parent and a worker were immense. The biggest problem was how to leave my children with house help while I worked nights or traveled for work, both local and abroad. One time, I was to travel to Kitui for a whole week to record programs for radio. My son was unwell with malaria symptoms, which worried me greatly. At only sixteen years of age, Victor was always doing things for people, helping or volunteering at the only home for the aged in Nairobi, Huruma Estate called Mji wa Huruma. He would go there to bathe and shave the old people who were terribly neglected. I was happy because that is what I did when I was young.

This day when I was to go to Kitui, I was at work when my neighbor fell suddenly ill. His wife who was young with three small children came to our house screaming. My son Victor, being who he is, ran out bare feet and assisted the sick man. He looked for transport and took him to Kenyatta, but the man was pronounced dead on arrival. My son came back so dejected, feeling sad. It could have been the trauma of a man he knew too well dying on him. The diagnosis revealed the man died of meningitis. Knowing how it can spread like wildfire, I worried about my son who had held the man all the way to hospital.

I left home for Kitui, but the boy was constantly on my mind. I left instructions that he should see the doctor. For two days I had no peace of mind at all. I called home every two hours. Luckily enough, his only symptom was the stress caused by watching a man die, leaving a wife and three young children behind. It might have had an effect on him, rekindling olden memories

The fact that I wanted the best for my sons could have turned me into a helicopter parent. But again, if my mother hadn't been one, I could have quit school altogether.

I have always been strict with my children. I punished them when they had erred, but we were best of friends when they didn't. I visited their schools and allowed the teachers to give them corporal punishment, but they had to do it in the way of discipline, not beating the hell out of them. I know non-African readers will think I'm a bad mother, but that is how we raise our African children. What I see in America where children talk back at their parents is not applicable in Africa. I guess it is all about culture.

Having seen what my mother did with teachers who had been mean to me, I understood that some teachers were not meant to handle children. Any teacher beating my child mercilessly had to contend with me, and I must say that I confronted quite a number of them. One particular incident was when children had to go to school during holidays for tuition. My son Tony didn't have a school uniform, as the one he had was totally torn. I was waiting to get money at the end of the month to buy him a new uniform when schools opened. Meanwhile, he could go to school for tuition in home clothes because I had paid the tuition money. This lady teacher Mildred kept beating him up and sending him out of class because he didn't dress up in uniform. On the third day, I went to school to confront the teacher and demanded my tuition money back. She ran as I followed her until she shakily opened the office and handed me my two thousand shillings back.

Holiday tuition was illegal anyway—just a way of teachers making extra income. She shouldn't have been sending my son away for lack of uniform after I paid what she wanted. I was there at school first thing in the morning come school opening day to square matters with the headteacher. I made sure she was transferred. My status as a well-known and respected person allowed me to hold a lot of sway in such matters. When it came to protecting my children, I was like a lioness with her cubs . . . exactly the way my own mother had been.

There was another challenge of smiling on the microphone, even when you were under stress. I talked about Stanley and how he hated me because he didn't understand why I wouldn't bow to his advances and yet I was single. At one time, the work I did most was to write letters of 'show cause why' more than the production and presentation I was supposed to do. We lived in the same area, and we would board the same Kenya Bus together to go to work in the morning.

Sometimes the bus would delay, and other times it would be too full for us to get on it. This meant that Stanley and I would be late to work together, but immediately after we entered through the gate, he would tell me that he was the boss, above the law and that I had to show cause why I was late. He then went to the office, and the first thing he did was write a letter to me, demanding a reply within two hours—the time I would still be in the studio. I used to cry as I worked, but as soon as I opened the microphone to say something on the air, I had to sound happy like nothing was going on.

Another challenge was when my father died. I received news of the death of my father through a colleague who had received the call at Broadcasting House while I was covering the international Nairobi trade fair at Jamhuri showground. We had passes for the show, and so she came to relieve me in doing the live broadcasts. I had gathered material for different current affairs programs, which I had to do before leaving. First, I presented the commercial program that was waiting, and then I went to Broadcasting House to prepare the current affairs programs before I went home to get ready to travel upcountry.

The following day, I tried to get means to travel home in vain. During the show days, the traffic in Nairobi is very congested, making traveling very difficult. My son Maxwell, who was ten years old at the time, wanted to travel with me. We couldn't find the means, but fortunately, I met Mr. Rajab Wellington Mwondi, the National Chairman, Central Organization of Trade Unions. He is my cousin and had left home that day very early before news of my father's death reached him. As soon as I told him, he told his driver to fuel the car and that we were going home. I had no words to thank him.

At my father's burial, there was a tug of war as to where he would be buried. They decided to bury him at my other mother's house because she had sons when my mother had only daughters who didn't matter those days. We quarreled and insulted each other with my brother and sisters from the other house, but by the burial day, we forgave each other.

I think my mother's passing and the circumstances around it were a bigger challenge. I received the news of my mother's death news at night when I was on transmission or continuity duty. I was in the studio on a Sunday night. Outside calls were never allowed to the studio extensions but I had friends all over. When my sister called after my mother died at ten o'clock at night, and she had to travel to Gambogi to get a call box, it was quarter to eleven. The lady at the switchboard was my friend, so she transferred the call to the studio in good faith.

I had gone to the village to see my ailing mother on Thursday that week, but I had to come back on Saturday to present Dunia Wiki Hii on Sunday morning and go back at night for my shift work. My mother was very sick. I hated to leave her, but duty called. I cried all the way to Nairobi, and so when I received my sister's call, it was not a big surprise, but all the same, I was shaken. I wanted to scream, but I couldn't. The whole world listening to the radio does not care what happens to the announcer. I had to keep smiling at the mic until I closed the station at midnight. On my way home, I passed Anunda Sakwa's house. He was my colleague but also a close friend. I told him to inform the bosses so they could see what to do with my shifts. I left very early the following day to go home. My mother's death still pains me to this day, twenty-eight years later.

I have always done things to surpass people who belittled me in life. God has been so faithful that they all come back, seeking a relationship with us. Although I lived in Nairobi all my life, I visited Hamisi occasionally, especially during funerals. Out of the ten Erude children, only one is still alive, and that is Jessica. All the boys are dead and gone, but I feel sad that it was meant to happen that way. As soon as they knew my school fees problem was over, they started coming, each blaming the other for what had happened to me. But just as the story of Joseph in the bible goes, that Juda was the only brother who said, "Let's not kill him. He is our brother", and made the brothers retrieve Joseph from the cistern and sold him. He became the most famous, as the Jews are his descendants. Jessica was one of very few who were sympathetic to my plight, together with my mother-in-law, Susan.

Back home in Tigoi, all my sisters are dead except for Truphena, and my brothers are all dead except Laban. My uncle Samuel died on September 3, 2007, twenty-one years after my father, who died on October 3, 1986. Lily lived to eighty-four and died in January of 2017. Of all the people I have lost, I still feel my mother's death fresh in my heart, although she died many years ago.

I have mentioned David Olocho several times, and I will have done a disservice to him if I didn't conclude his story. I have related how he helped me without knowing who I was. I came to learn about him being a member of my Maragoli community very late. They always say one turn deserves another. Although he was a senior civil servant, he got himself into a problem of not filing his taxes. At that time, ethnicity and a certain community getting advantaged over others was gaining ground.

He learned to play golf with white people whom he had worked with when he was a District Commissioner. This made him unpopular because somebody thought he was being sympathetic to colonialists. All his salary was attached for six months, and he didn't have a way of paying rent or fueling his car—not even enough to buy food. When he confided in me, I invited him to stay with us in the house I shared with Sally and eat the little we had. The house became enough when Sally moved out to live with her uncle in the same estate. With time, he and I became more than just friends.

Olocho encouraged me to know the Lord deeper. He taught me how not to say anything against children because it becomes a curse. I was very much attached to him.

His death devastated me. It happened when I was taking a stroll with him one day. When he suddenly stopped along the way, I thought he just wanted to 'stand against the hedge' as men often do, and so I took a few steps ahead. When I looked back, he was lying on the ground. I tried to resuscitate him in vain. I was therefore surprised when stories went around that I killed him and carried his body to the road to pretend he died on his own. I am forever grateful to his sons who understood the whole story and knew I had taken good care of their father.

I wanted my boys to get what I did not get. There is this notion in African society that children raised by single mothers become delinquent. I didn't want that to happen to my children.

There was a time when all four of my bigger boys were in high school, and that meant more school fees to pay. I became a member of two very strong women's groups. These groups would put money together at the beginning of the year and start 'shylocking' (lending out money for interest). The money would be brought back at the end of the year for dividing among members. I would get a total of between sixty and seventy thousand Kenya shillings (600–700 US dollars). With this money I paid all the tuition I was required to pay in a year for each boy. Thank God tuition was still less than ten thousand shillings a year per child, but all the same, very hard to come by. This means that none of my children was sent home for lack of payment. Much later, the boys complained to me that I always paid fees in full instead of leaving them to be sent home at least for a while for a break from the grueling school routine.

My firstborn, Victor, went to Aquinas high school. He then proceeded to go to college for Tours and Hotels Management. He worked for a while in Nairobi, but his mind was set on business. He saved all the money to buy equipment for making French fries, popularly known in Kenya as chips. His best friend's mother had wanted to raise chicken, a project that did not go well. She then threw away the chicken house, which my boys went to pick, cleaned it up, painted it and made it as good as new. They erected it next to our house in Civil Servants Estate. They used to peel potatoes by themselves; they had bought a chipper and fryer, and also a warmer.

The business started gradually but after three months, people were waiting in long lines for the food. My son has always been a hard worker. It may be that I placed importance on him as being the man of the house after the death of his father, although he was only four years old. He used to get up at four o'clock to go to the farmers' market to buy potatoes and scallions for making *samosa*. After one year, he was calling a van to deliver ten bags of potatoes and didn't have to go to the market in the morning.

Victor had set his life bar very high, and he wanted to realize his dream. In January, 1996, he left his café in the care of his brothers and went to Britain to look for opportunities. Things didn't work out well for him, so I advised him to come back home. In July of the same year, he met a God-fearing man called Patrick who advised him to try the USA. November of the same year, he went to the US. Meanwhile, Sylvester was completing his Bachelor of Education degree at Nairobi University at Kikuyu campus after completing his high school education at Upper Hill. As much as he wanted to study Law, he was only given education, and more so to do English instead of French, which he had already mastered. The Kenyan education system was messed up then, and you had to belong to a certain ethnicity to get to do a good professional degree. He graduated in 1997. He was posted at Goibei Girls high school, where he taught for three months only. Victor later invited him to the US and I accompanied him because I had missed Victor very much. He went straight to college for his master's degree.

Felix was in love with engineering but was never given a chance to follow his dreams for reasons I stated before. He went to Starehe Boys Center. Instead of his preferred course, he was taken to Kabete campus to study Bcom. He studied it for three years and decided he didn't like it. He also left for The States in 1999 together with Maxwell who had completed his high school at Aquinas. All my boys went to Western Illinois University. Victor made sure that they all went to college as he worked to cater to their needs before he also went to college. Felix started his engineering program afresh while Maxwell and Sylvester went into I/T.

Victor putting his brothers before himself reminded me of our neighbors in Hamisi. The man ran away with another woman, leaving his wife to fend for the children. The mother became so depressed that it drove her to insanity. The elder brother, who had at least gone to school and found a job, neglected his mother and two small brothers. These two boys used to work on people's farms to get food. When their mother died, they remained on their own. The bigger of the two brothers worked menial jobs to see his youngest brother through school. When the younger brother got a job with National Social Security Fund, he took his older brother, who was now twenty-eight, to primary school. He later went to high school, graduated, and got a job. It is never too late for one to seek knowledge.

The boys in Kenya haven't done badly. Tony works with Kenya Airways, and Byron is a mighty man of God and my prayer partner. Apart from my six boys, I have a daughter,

Lilian whom I adopted and gave her my name. She is a teacher and married to a pastor of the Quaker church. My life is good and I praise God every day.

THE END

www.ingramcontent.com/pod-product-compliance
Lightning Source LLC
Chambersburg PA
CBHW020905080526
44589CB00011B/456